DO YOU MA
THESE MIST

- INTERCEDE with an S instead of the C?
- MORTGAGE without the T?
- OUTRAGEOUS without the E?
- MISSPELLING with only one S?

SIX MINUTES A DAY TO PERFECT SPELLING will help you eliminate such mistakes forever by teaching you to SEE THE WORD, THINK THE WORD, FEEL THE WORD, SAY THE WORD, and BUILD THE WORD.

"Whether in our program of special classes for adults at New York University—where he introduced the first course in spelling to be offered at this level—or on television to a 'spelling class' of 2,000 registered students, Harry Shefter teaches with zest and wit and freshness of attack on old problems."

—*Paul A. McGhee, former Dean of
General Education, New York University*

Books by Harry Shefter

Faster Reading Self-Taught
How to Prepare Talks and Oral Reports
Shefter's Guide to Better Compositions
Shortcuts to Effective English
Six Minutes a Day to Perfect Spelling
A Teacher's Guide to Supplementary Reading
Teaching Aids for 40 Enriched Classics

Published by POCKET BOOKS

Six Minutes a Day to Perfect Spelling

REVISED EDITION

Harry Shefter

Professor of English
New York University

A KANGAROO BOOK
PUBLISHED BY POCKET BOOKS NEW YORK

To Evelyn and our two ladies—Barbara and Sharon Ann

 POCKET BOOKS, a Simon & Schuster division of
GULF & WESTERN CORPORATION
1230 Avenue of the Americas, New York, N.Y. 10020

ISBN: 0-671-81281-5

First Pocket Books printing (revised edition) July, 1976

3rd printing

Trademarks registered in the United States and other countries.

Printed in the U.S.A.

Contents

You and Spelling

If you have a spelling problem, you cannot be identified simply on the basis of how you look or what you do. You may be a casually dressed student, smartly groomed secretary, bulky business executive, dignified college instructor, energetic mechanic, or harried housewife. In fact, if you never wrote another word, only your old friends and associates would ever know that you had a weakness in spelling!

What I am really saying is that, barring a serious physical or emotional disorder, it is more than likely that you are not a special case. You have lots of company. When you went to grade school, over 60 percent of your classmates worried about their spelling. If you were graduated from a secondary school and then went on to higher education, you will be interested to know that a national survey conducted among colleges and universities revealed that more than 25 percent of the students, seniors as well as freshmen, had *serious* spelling problems—some missing words as easy as "sense." In short, whether you are very young or quite mature, whether you left school early to get a job or attended long enough to get several degrees, neither your educational background nor your native intelligence has anything necessarily to do with your ability to spell correctly.

Here's something else. You are concerned about your

spelling, as you should be, but you never quite get around to doing anything about it, except in a haphazard way. Perhaps you've tried to memorize rules, write words out countless times as practice, study long lists of "demons," play "find-the-incorrect-word" games, even fearfully enter spelling bees in the vague hope that somehow you would improve. But you haven't improved because all of these methods are of little value in a long-range plan.

What you need is an organized, fresh attack. That's what you're going to find in this book. The suggested techniques, *if you use them*, are guaranteed to bring you success—and I do not say this recklessly!

A Greek immigrant, within less than a year after his arrival in this country, was helped to master a list of "Two Hundred Most Frequently Misspelled Words" under the word-a-day plan described in the following pages. When I say "master," I mean he proved he had the words under control for good in frequent writing experiences during the course of his training. What is equally interesting is that while Mr. Costas was concentrating on the selected list he was also picking up numerous other words and adding them to his private collection.

The system has worked with people of all ages. A nine-year-old boy, the son of a colleague of mine, learned how to stop embarrassing his learned father. Twenty-three native-born Americans, ranging in age from twenty-three to fifty-seven, members of the first class in spelling ever given on the university level, were shown how to get rid of practically all of their troublemakers in less than six months. A television audience of approximately sixty thousand people wrote enthusiastic letters about the methods presented before the cameras, and asked that the suggestions be put into book form. As a matter of fact, that's one of the main reasons why *Six Minutes a Day to Perfect Spelling* was written.

I've told you all this to convince you that you have it in your power to rid yourself of, once and for all, your spelling problems. However, a word of warning must be inserted here. You will hear it again and again as we work together. If you merely read each chapter carefully, you will not be any better off at the end than when you started. That is, if you only *read*, and do not *do*. You will have to cooperate; there's no question about that. But, happily, it's only *Six Minutes a Day to Perfect Spelling!*

HARRY SHEFTER

· I ·

Good Spellers Are Made, Not Born!

Please write your name in pencil below:

Kathy Killingsworth

You just wrote your name.

When was the last time you misspelled it? You probably can't remember. Spelling your name is automatic. You do it without thought, without hesitation, knowing it will come out right. *There is no reason, then, why you can't do the same with any word in the English language.*

I'm going to show you how. That's *my* job. I will also tell you how to practice, so that correct spelling can stay with you forever. That will be *your* job. We'll work as a team, and sooner than you dare expect, you will be able to spell any word you want as easily and automatically as you do your name.

Why does a person always spell his own name correctly? The reason is simply that he has made the words in his name a part of him. He has reduced their spelling to the habit level. Mind you; this is as true of Aleksandra Trzettizorriskaya (a student of mine some years ago) as it is of John Brown, Jack Smith, or you.

It stands to reason, then, that your spelling will improve when you learn to treat other words the same way. Reduce them to the habit level. Make them a part of you.

Don't worry about long nights of study devoted to impossible-to-remember rules and procedures. This is not that kind of book. All you will need is *Six Minutes a Day* of your time. All you will have to learn is five simple steps:

SEE THE WORD!

THINK THE WORD!

FEEL THE WORD!

SAY THE WORD!

BUILD THE WORD!

That's all: Six minutes a day and five steps.

Let's begin by clearing away some bad spelling alibis. A popular one is that weakness in spelling runs in families. Grandpa had lots of trouble, Papa used to chew the pencil to bits when he wrote, and naturally Junior can't be expected to do any better. Nonsense! Each slipped into the same bad habits, and not one bothered to break them.

Perhaps someone has said to you:

"How can I ever learn to spell? The sounds in the language don't seem to agree with the letters. I write *enough*. The *gh* sounds like an *f*. Then I find that in *phone* the *ph* is also an *f* sound. When I get to *often*, the *f* is an *f*, but the *t* is nothing!"

This kind of poor speller blames our language for his troubles. There are too many silent letters, he says; too many peculiar combinations that don't spell the way they sound.

He seems to have a point. Consider how the English language grew. The ancient history of the British Isles is the record of one invasion after another. About three thousand years ago, the first invaders, variously known as Celts, Gaels, or Britons, made their appearance in Scotland, Ireland, Wales, and England. Although these tribes stayed over nine hundred years, they left little evidence of their language. Less than 1 percent of the contents of a modern unabridged dictionary can be traced to these earliest inhabitants.

About 55 B.C., Caesar's legions started to bully their way into England. Strangely, however, the strong Latin and Greek influence on English did not occur in the four hundred years of Roman occupation, but came during the revival of learning in the Renaissance period and from eighteenth-century classical scholars like Dr. Samuel Johnson.

After the Romans, Teutonic hordes—Angles, Saxons, and Jutes—came storming in. By A.D. 500, the remnants of the original Britons had been driven to obscure regions, and Anglo-Saxon became the foundation of the language we use. Words such as *wisdom, beggar, weakling,* and *ownership,* while containing some unclear vowel sounds and doubled consonants, would not have presented very serious problems.

However, in 1066, William the Conqueror's Frenchmen surged across the Channel and began to force new words into the language. *Bailiff, mortgage, embellish, chamois, camouflage,* and *technique* are typical words of French ancestry that contain silent letters that baffle poor spellers.

A few centuries later, the delayed Roman influence set in. Examples like *aquarium, asterisk, achievement, statistician,* and *chiropractor* show the kind of "jawbreakers," as some call them, that began to appear in English. Often mere length of a word or unusual letter combinations are enough to floor the timid. "Looks too tough!" we say.

Even after the thirteen colonies had become the United States, and had adopted the language of their forefathers, borrowing went on freely. We reached into the Scandinavian countries and took *ransack, dahlia, flounder,* and *sleigh,* among others. *Macaroni, motto, dilettante,* and *colonnade* are but a few of the words Italy gave us.

From Spain, we appropriated *barbecue, bronco, lariat, sombrero,* and others. Hebrew, Arabic, Indian, Persian, Slavic, American Indian, African, and Chinese are additional languages that enriched our vocabulary, but added to our spelling problems.

Is it any wonder that English has no pattern? We take foreign words with complicated letter formations, don't bother to simplify them, and dump them right into the hopper. Then off we go on another merry spelling jamboree, or so it seems.

But if this were the basic cause of our troubles, we would just throw up our hands and hope for the best. Actually, scientific studies prove that through the years *most spelling mistakes are made with simple, everyday words.*

The classic collection of frequently misspelled words, found in every grade school speller and called "100 Spelling Demons," is a good example. Take a look at this list at the beginning of the Appendix (page 147). Not one of the demons looks frightening, does it? Yet these words, and others like them, give poor spellers most of their headaches.

Poor spelling is, therefore, neither inherited nor completely created by the structure of the language. How *does* it come about? Almost always, the trouble starts early in life *and becomes a bad habit.*

To be analytical for a moment, here are the stories of real people who let themselves fall into misspelling traps. Each is typical of how a poor speller is made, not born.

The Case of Mr. A.

He was introduced to the mystery of the written word by a rather grim-faced schoolteacher. The weekly spelling tests became moments of sheer horror. Poor marks increased his sense of failure. After a while, he unconsciously began to resist the whole annoying business. He fought back by deliberately showing that he didn't care. A certain amount of attention came his way because of his difficulty.

To live up to his reputation, young A. developed misspelling into a running joke on himself. When his weakness was exposed, he would laugh sheepishly, shake his head in pretended defiance, and lamely mumble, "Never could get the hang of it!" Today, although he is a fairly successful salesman, Mr. A. is secretly very much embarrassed about his spelling problems and knows they may some day cost him advancement.

The Case of Mr. D.

He left school early to open a small store selling automobile accessories. Last year, the fourth branch in a modestly growing chain was introduced. This intelligent, rising businessman is an official in the local Kiwanis, has become prominent in church affairs, and two weeks ago was invited to join a committee to draft a new city charter. Because this is the first time his writing and speaking abilities will come under the public eye, he's worried. Up to now, mispronunciations and misspellings have never been too important. Miss Corbett, his secretary, has been discreet about notes from his desk that came to her attention. She quietly revised errors like "probly, fillum, usialy"—all caused by incorrect pronunciations. Now, however, Mr. D. risks open exposure of his slovenly speech and writing. Accurate spelling and proper pronunciation go hand in hand, *and one does wash the other*. Our disturbed friend will have to decline the invitation. Until he has improved his verbal skills, he'll have to keep his weaknesses to himself.

The Case of Miss B.

She is a junior executive in an advertising agency. Everyone predicts a bright future for her. Although her record in college was brilliant, she constantly had trouble with the English courses. The instructors complained that they could not read her work because of her terrible handwriting. And carelessness in this respect led her to sloppy spelling habits. She would become confused when asked whether a particular letter should be "i" or "e," "a" or "o." Now a question that haunts her is: "Will my spelling weakness eventually cost me my job?"

The Case of Mrs. C.

This lady takes great pride in her sparkling new home in the suburbs. Because she likes to entertain and take part in club activities, she often finds it necessary to send notes and letters. But she dreads the task because it becomes a major undertaking. An hour or so with the dictionary and a floor littered with discarded sheets of stationery have become the symbols of this ordeal. Mrs. C. has just never learned to *see* a word with her *mind* as well as with her eyes. She needs to be trained to visualize, so that the letters will not form a filmy blur and spelling will not become an emotional catastrophe.

The Case of Mary E.

She is suffering from a serious brain injury. Talking and writing are very trying experiences. She sees words as you would if you held a paper up to a mirror. Often the letters become jumbled. Only her doctor, through his medical skill and knowledge, can be of any real assistance to her.

There they are. Each is an exhibit in a gallery of poor spellers. One has lost his confidence; another can't say the word right, much less spell it; the third let her slipshod penmanship get her into trouble; the fourth hasn't learned to get a mental picture of the word. Yes, there are good reasons why they can't spell and even better reasons why they should improve. Only Mary E. needs more than a fresh start. The rest can rid themselves of their spelling problems by breaking bad habits and substituting good ones.

You've just reviewed the causes of poor spelling. Whatever yours are, get moving in the right direction today. There are lots of things in your favor. For instance, your personal list of "spelling demons" with which you will have to work isn't so long as you think. I dare say that if you could remember and write down the words you always misspell you'd come up with fewer than fifty or sixty. Second, you really want to do something about your spelling. Otherwise you wouldn't even be reading this. And certainly, if in a short time you can look any word squarely in the eye, it will be worth the effort you make in following the suggestions outlined here.

Let's get down to business. Let's look at the tricks of the trade.

· II ·

See the Word!

We can all see with our minds as well as with our eyes.
For instance, right now you would have no difficulty creating a mental picture of your best friend, the room you sleep in, or the details and colors of your favorite outfit. If you wanted to, you could also recall the sign over a restaurant you have visited, a striking roadside warning, or the slogan that identifies a product frequently advertised. It doesn't matter whether the images are objects or words; your mind can help you "look" at them whenever you please.

The ability to use the "mind's eye," as Shakespeare called it, is characteristic of all good spellers and is, as a matter of fact, one of their major trade secrets. Of course, once they have reduced the spelling of a word to the habit level, they do not need any extra help with it. Their hand simply writes the word automatically. But when they are in doubt or want to check a spelling, they can create a mental picture of a word at will. When they do this, they actually *see the word* and then proceed to trace the image orally or on paper.

Because you already have the ability to see with your mind, you can train yourself to apply it to the spelling of words you have not yet reduced to the habit level. It's a must! Without developing this technique, your progress will be very slow. With it, you will be able to remove a roadblock to improvement.

Start your first training session immediately. Turn this

book over and look at the back cover. Note the large *6* in the phrase "6 Minutes a Day" printed in red at the bottom. Be sure you are seated comfortably and are completely relaxed. Get set to concentrate.

All right. Try to make your mind a blank. *Stare very hard at the number and words for ten seconds*. Just stare—try not to think—do nothing else.

Now look away toward some dark surface—the wall, floor, that old couch cover. *Count five*. The image of at least the number should reappear on the blank area. Practice until this happens regularly.

Try this method with other arrangements: a series of colored circles, a strip from the Sunday comics, a design from a gaudy sport shirt. Stare at the pattern for ten seconds, look away, count five, and try to recreate the image on another surface.

After you train yourself to throw a picture with your mind, try it with words. We'll use **calenDAR** as the first example.

If you have trouble with the word, you probably misspell it at the **DAR** syllable. The fact is that people rarely spell a word so badly that it cannot be recognized. Usually, it is one particular part, or only one letter, that causes the spelling problem. Therefore, focus your attention on the part of the word *you* always misspell—the difficult part for you. Your objective is to get rid of the distorted image you have in your mind and to replace it with a clear and correct one.

Write the word in this manner:

calen DAR

Now the difficult part stands out. Look at this image for ten seconds. Remember: just stare. Let the picture sink in.

Again, try to *see* the image on another surface. Count five. Make sure the difficult part shows up most clearly.

On a piece of paper, write out calenDAR rapidly, "looking" at the picture of the word with your mind's eye all the while. Repeat the whole procedure three times.

*   *   *

Here are some other devices you can use to set up the image:

1. Try colored crayon for the difficult part, and plain ink or pencil for the rest of the letters.

2. Separate the parts, and underline the difficulty:

   cal en dar

3. Circle the key part:

   calen (dar)

4. Use the number 2 to remind you that certain words are always written in two parts:

   all 2 right

Spellick #1

If you think you've never seen the word "spellick" before, you are right. It was invented for this book. *Six Minutes a Day to Perfect Spelling* is a complete course in itself. The only additional tools you need are a dictionary, a pencil, and some paper, things you should already own. There are, however, some other very useful tools that you can build for yourself . . . if you have the time and, more important, if you have the desire to get ahead as fast as possible. We have called these extra devices *spellicks,* the gimmicks or special tricks in this business of learning to spell. *Spellicks* are separated from the rest of the instruction because they are extras rather than musts. But *spellicks* are the *power tools* of spelling. Use them if you possibly can. Here is *spellick* number one:

Cut a piece of *yellow* cardboard about two feet long and about six inches wide. Use this as the background. Cut other pieces of cardboard of the same color into strips about one foot long and three inches wide. On one such strip, in *black letters,* print the word you are studying at the moment. As you print, make the letters of the difficult part twice the size of the others. Now you have an excellent tool for **seeing the word.** The black on yellow will greatly sharpen the image. Just lean the background card against a solid object like a book end, and place the word card in front of it.

Of course, you continue the process of staring at the image for ten seconds, looking away, counting five, trying to create a mind picture, and then writing the word out rapidly as you visualize it.

SEE THE WORD with these:

ar**GUM**ent	**ILL**iterate	qua**RR**el
bar**GAIN**	jud**GM**ent	re**COMMEND**
se**PAR**ate	kero**SENE**	**SECRET**ary
DEStroy	le**IS**ure	temp**ERA**ture
en**VEL**ope	man**AGE**	**UN**able
femi**NINE**	ne**CESS**ary	**VINE**gar
gr**ATE**ful	o**CC**asion	w**HIST**le
hand**KER**chief	**PART**ner	

CAUTION: Do not try to master the list above in one day. Rather, test yourself with the diagnostic paragraph prepared for this chapter to determine which words need further study. Save these until you have covered Chapter VII. Then give each word you missed "The Treatment."

As a review of this chapter, we have prepared a paragraph containing every key word mentioned in the explanatory material. Naturally, the real test of your ability to spell correctly is in your own writing when you are not deliberately being careful. Therefore, we have used the paragraph form, rather than a list, to make the situation as natural as possible.

These essays are not offered as literary gems. The need to keep them short and at the same time have them contain a special group of particular words creates a problem. Nevertheless, the occasional near-nonsense sentence should not interfere with your main objective, which is to use these paragraphs as a test of how much you have learned!

The best way to test yourself on the paragraph below —or any other ones that will appear in the chapters that follow—is to ask someone to read aloud to you as you write. If you do it this way, make certain that the reader dictates at the proper tempo and in appropriate phrasing.

You will probably have to practice with your reader for a time in order to develop the speed that will enable you to write smoothly, without rushing.

Should you be unable to use a reader, you can still manage. If you must work on the material by yourself, simply rewrite it. Look at the key words (those in **boldface**) as you get to them in the sentences *only long enough to identify them,* but not long enough to help you spell them. Try to see the difficult part of each troublesome word *in your mind* while you are writing. This is admittedly not the best way to test yourself, but if you exercise self-control, it will work.

Use the blank spaces below the paragraph to jot down the words you misspelled. These should be given "The Treatment" *after* you have covered the first seven chapters.

Diagnostic Paragraph

If you wish to study a typical **feminine argument,** I **recommend** that you visit a **bargain** counter. You will see how two shoppers can sometimes **manage** to get into a **quarrel** over even a **handkerchief.** In the **judgment** of each unwilling **partner,** she simply must have the article for her **leisure** moments. On one **occasion,** I saw the **temperature** of a **secretary** go up as if it were lighted **kerosene.** She had picked up a **calendar** in an **envelope,** but a bystander had been **unable** to resist reaching for it, too. One would have thought both were **illiterate** from the looks washed in **vinegar** that passed between them. Each surely would have been **grateful** if she had been able to **destroy** the other. It looked for a moment as if a **whistle** would have to be blown to **separate** the pair, but a **saleslady** made everything **all right** when she pointed out that the item was not even for sale.

Handkerchief

Judgment

Vinegar

A word or two about tests in general, and spelling tests in particular. In most areas of information, it is customary to use an examination to measure general knowledge in the field. In school subjects, for example, the traditional 65 percent or higher indicates satisfactory achievement. Similarly, a mark of 85 percent might be excellent on a state professional or civil service examination.

But such grades in a spelling test would be meaningless! They would indicate only the percentage of words that need further study. The speller cannot be satisfied with 85, 90 or 98 percent. He must strive for 100 percent _every time_.

You will not, therefore, find any tests here designed merely to allow you to get a score. All the sentences and paragraphs at the ends of chapters or in the appendix are there to help you learn two things:

> the words you still have to study,
> the words you have already mastered.

Toying with long lists of deliberately misspelled examples of errors or picking out the correct forms from several possibilities is an utter waste of time. In fact, it is dangerous to concentrate your attention on the *wrong* spelling at any time. Your mind may not choose to remember the right one the next time you have to use the word! For this reason, there are no distorted spellings or useless tests in this book.

SEE THE WORD,
now . . .

Think the Word!

Look very quickly at each of the ten words listed below. In the space provided, write the first thing that pops into your mind. Try to make your response as automatic as you can.

aunt	*uncle*	fear	*Scared*
blue	*Sky*	girl	*Boy*
care	*yourself*	head	*Foot*
duty	*work*	iron	*Hate*
ease	*Vacation*	June	*hot*

Now examine each combination, the original word and the one you inserted. What made *aunt* suggest _____ to you? Think about it for a moment. If you wrote the name of a person in the space, isn't she the one you like best, or possibly never could tolerate? If you wrote *sad* after *blue,* isn't it that the color depresses you for one reason or another? If you put *chair* or *couch* after *ease,* you probably identify relaxation with a favorite piece of furniture. But no matter what you wrote down, by filling in the spaces you participated in what psychologists call an "association of ideas."

This term applies to a very basic mental process. Your mind sometimes helps you remember things by establishing **BONDS** between details that have meaning only to you. That's why the strains of a familiar melody can bring back a picture of a wonderful evening you once enjoyed; why you'll reject a certain kind of food because it makes you think, perhaps subconsciously, of those harrowing mornings you spent on the high chair, struggling with your persistent mother: why the number *sixteen* may mean a dreamy birthday party to a girl.

In the ability of your mind to associate lies the key to another secret of good spelling. You have learned how to get a mental picture of the difficult part of a word. Now if you can place a mental string around your finger in addition to the image in your mind, the result will be startling. When you tie in the problem syllable with an instantly recalled idea, you will have another strong aid toward the proper spelling of a word. The secret is simply to form a **BOND.**

Let's go back to *calendar,* the example we used to point out how advisable it is to *see* the word with the *mind* as well as the *eye.* The *a* between the *d* and *r* is the trouble-maker. Now invent a statement that creates a **BOND** between the difficult part and an easily remembered idea.

For example, suppose you were to associate the difficult part of *calendar* with the initials of the organization known as the Daughters of the American Revolution (DAR); your statement might go this way:

According to the calen**DAR,** the **DAR** will meet this week.

There it is. You have now created an association that will give you further help in fixing the difficult part of the word in your mind. Inventing **BONDS** can be an entertaining game. The rules are simple:

1. Set up the association.

2. Make it as silly or as unusual as you can. Oddly enough, we tend to remember our own word inventions, however nonsensical, more readily than we do someone else's logic.

3. Try to combine this association with an image in your mind as explained in the previous chapter. See the word, **and** think the word! Thus, you make the difficult part of the word both the basis for the **IMAGE** and the association for the **BOND.**

4. Once you've decided on a good combination, study it for ten seconds, look away toward another surface, *see and think* the problem syllable, and then write the whole word out rapidly.

Take a look at these additional examples. After you have become thoroughly familiar with the method, gradually make up a list of your own.

1. It is **VILE** to allow special pri**VILE**ge.
2. The suit on the **SERGEANT** looked like **SERGE** on an **ANT.**
3. She screamed, **"EEE!"** as she passed the c**EmEt**Ery.
4. The **VILLAIN** enjoyed his **VILLA IN** the hills.
5. Scientists **LABOR** in a **LABOR**atory.
6. **GM** (General Motors) sent an acknowled**GM**ent.
7. Every **AGE** has its tr**AGE**dy.
8. You **GAIN** when you buy a bar**GAIN.**
9. My **PROF** is called **PROF**essor Gordon.
10. He lost his **TEMPER AT** the rise in **TEMPER-AT**ure.
11. Don't **MAR** your writing with bad gram**MAR.**
12. Draw **ALL** the lines par**ALL**el.

13. There was constant rePETition of his PET phrase.
14. TEN times later, his persisTENce was rewarded.
15. She flew into a RAGE at his outRAGEous remarks.
16. EMMA was in a dilEMMA.
17. When I think of FeBRuary, I say, "BR!"
18. It was an ERA of great litERAture.
19. The princiPAL is my PAL.
20. You RILE me with your sacRILEgious remarks.
21. StationERy is for a lettER.
22. When he ATE, he was grATEful.
23. "ACH!" There goes the parACHute.
24. My skin shows resisTANce to TAN.
25. He would sooner DIE than be obeDIEnt.

It may occur to you at this point that some of the **BONDS** don't seem to help you very much. This is as it should be. The bonds must be made up *by you!* You will remember what *you* have created far better than something thought of by another person.

Diagnostic Paragraph

Early in **February,** an **acknowledgment** written on official **stationery** came from the **laboratory.** By this time, the police chief's **temperature** was at the boiling point. The **tragedy** of the torn **parachute,** discovered by the **persistence** of Sergeant Bristol, remained unsolved. The **villain** was still at large, and there wasn't even a **principal** suspect. But the chief had faced a **dilemma** before. In **grammar** that a **professor** would never use and a minister might call **sacrilegious,** he ordered his men to search every part of the city, even the **cemetery,** and to break down the **resistance** of anyone brought in. The **outrageous** crime had no **parallel** in the **literature** of **murder,** but it is the **privilege** of a seldom **grateful** public to demand results. Police chiefs are **obedient** to a public mood, and in this case, the public, fearing a **repetition** of the crime, was in no mood to **bargain.**

Tragedy
principal
dilemma
resistance
privilege

AGAIN, CAUTION: Do not try to master the words you misspell in the test paragraph until you have covered Chapter VII.

Spellick #2

If you have no one available to dictate these paragraphs, there is still a way to solve the problem. Get yourself a tape or cassette recording machine. If you can't buy it, perhaps you can borrow one. Then you can simply record the material in this and other chapters. Thereafter, you can play back the paragraphs at your leisure, and write as you listen. You will find the page numbers of all the summary paragraphs in the index. You can use the recorder for the diagnostic sentences there, too.

There are many advantages to such an arrangement. The fact that you hear *your own voice* dictating should help you remember. You can play the tape or record as often as and whenever you like, stop when you please, and even make up essays of your own for further tests. If you use this suggestion, be careful to observe these cautions for the actual recording:

1. Speak clearly into the microphone, pronouncing extra-carefully. Do not leave out any syllables or letters.

2. Break up the sentences into phrases. For example: "Early in February—an acknowledgment—written on official stationery—came from the laboratory—"

3. Read slowly, pausing long enough after each phrase to allow yourself time to write it. You can accustom yourself to the proper timing by practicing writing sentences as you read them aloud. When you think you have the tempo set, and you begin to record, *allow a few more seconds at each break.*

4. Identify each paragraph after the recording. Write the page number of the paragraph on a label placed on the container of the tape or cassette.

5. If you aren't satisfied with a particular recording, *do it over*. Unless you feel comfortable as you listen, the recorded material will be more of a hindrance than a help!

So far you have learned to SEE THE WORD in your mind and THINK THE WORD by association. Now let's turn to the third important method of solving your spelling problems.

· IV ·

Feel the Word!

Have you ever watched a blind person become familiar with a strange object? He goes over the outline of the figure carefully and slowly. *Through his fingers,* he is memorizing the shape. When he feels something similar again, his sense of touch will immediately identify it. In fact, this is the way a blind person learns to read Braille. But all of us have the ability to "think" and "see" with our fingers. Here are two illustrations.

You sit in a darkened movie theater. As you watch the film, you hear clicking sounds nearby. You are puzzled, but when the lights go on, you discover a woman putting her knitting away. Her *fingers* have been busy in the dark while her mind was concentrating on the screen.

One morning you are late. As you dash down the steps, your fingers feverishly make a knot in your tie. Your mind, already forming excuses for tardiness, doesn't spend a second's thought on your tie. Your *fingers* are doing the thinking.

Or let me remind you about the signature you wrote on the first page. You didn't think about it. You let your *fingers* take charge. Your mind was probably wondering why you were asked to do the job.

There are many things you do almost entirely by reflex. The patterns of behavior are so habitual that your mind often operates in a secondary capacity. It has such a clear picture of the necessary movements and such a strong association with the proper reactions that the physical process becomes prompt, efficient, and almost unthinking.

You know how to **SEE THE WORD.** You know how to **THINK THE WORD.** Learn how to **FEEL THE WORD** and spelling will also become one of your mechanically perfect skills.

This physical attack upon words is designed to force the hand to do most of the work of spelling. It is another step in enabling you to write any word as casually as you do your signature.

Try this experiment. Write the number *19836* on a blank piece of paper. Put your finger on each digit and trace it, saying it aloud as you trace. Do this three times. Turn the paper over, and write the original number once more, but as you do, say aloud, *12345*. If you can write one number while saying another, you have proved that your hand can be taught to spell automatically.

This skill is particularly useful for words that contain more than one difficult part. A *bond* or *image* may not be enough to eliminate all the trouble spots.

Take the word **PSYCHOLOGY,** for example. A poor speller may forget that it begins with a *p* or that it contains a *y* and *ch*. It is therefore possible to make several errors. The attack must be on an overall basis. You must *feel* the *entire* word and be able to write it mechanically.

Use this system:

1. On a piece of paper, write the word in large, well-

rounded, *script* letters. About twice the size of your normal handwriting should be sufficient.

2. Place the pen or pencil you have used aside and, **with your finger** directly touching the letters, slowly **trace** the word, softly repeating aloud each letter as you trace it.

3. Allow no break in the rhythm. Your arm should swing along, not stopping its motion until it has completed the word. Dot the *i* or cross the *t,* if there is one.

4. Do this three times. Start carefully, and gradually increase the pace until it is very much like the speed at which you normally write.

5. After you have been able to sweep through the word confidently, without pausing, turn the paper over. **This is very important. Say anything aloud as you write out the word.** Repeat your name and address, or recite a favorite bit of poetry, or simply count. You want to grasp the word in a physical sense. The hand, not the mind, must do the spelling. By talking as you write, you force yourself to make the process automatic.

6. If you make the slightest mistake, repeat the exercise until your *hand* spells the word. Remember: use your finger to trace. Do not use a pen or pencil.

Here are a few more words that contain problems in several places. They can be handled best by the tracing method.

minimum

campaign

ridiculous

guardian

bureau

ascertain

memorandum

mortgage

guarantee

acknowledge

After a while, you will find that you can combine tracing with the two other techniques of *seeing* and *thinking*. Thus, if you must think about the spelling, it will help rather than hinder the writing.

Here is an easy way to combine the three steps you have learned so far:

1. Construct the image in your mind as suggested in the second chapter.
2. Prepare a **BOND** for the difficult part or parts of the word.
3. Trace the word *with your finger* three times.
4. Write it rapidly *as you look at the image in your mind,* and *repeat the bond aloud.* In this way, you will be **seeing the word, thinking the word,** and **feeling the word** all at once.

If you can master this four-step technique, 90 percent of your spelling troubles will be over.

Diagnostic Paragraph

Lucy looked at Mr. Forbes, her **guardian.** She felt that the terms of the **mortgage** were **ridiculous,** and she clearly recalled the **memorandum** the head of the housing **bureau** had sent to her. He had strongly urged some sort of **guarantee** of payments, so that the risks would be at a **minimum.** She realized she would first have to **ascertain** what **psychology** would work best before she could start a **campaign** to force Mr. Forbes to **acknowledge** the justice of her claim.

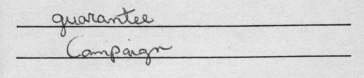

guarantee

Campaign

REMINDER: Add the words you misspelled during the dictation of the diagnostic paragraph to the list you are reserving for "The Treatment" *after* you have covered the first seven chapters.

SEE THE WORD!
THINK THE WORD!
FEEL THE WORD!
and . . .

· V ·

Say the Word!

Here's an old-time vaudeville joke, but there's more than a laugh buried in it.

A man goes into a restaurant and sits down at a table.

"I'll have some **kidley** stew," he says.

"Pardon, sir," suggests the waiter, "but don't you mean **kidney** stew?"

"I said **kidley** stew, **did'l** I?" replies the man.

It is very common for people to be entirely unaware of the spoken mistakes they make. These people haven't learned to listen to themselves talk. Unfortunately, oral errors are often transferred to written words. Many misspellings come directly from faulty pronunciation.

You tend to write the way you speak. Examine these:

SURPRISE   **FILM**
CAVALRY   **JEWELRY**

Say each one aloud. Try to listen to yourself as you speak. If you have trouble concentrating on your voice, use this simple device. Stand a few inches away from a wall. Hold your hands behind your ears and parallel to the wall. As you talk, you will hear the sounds as if they were coming over a microphone.

29

Now that you have pronounced the words, look them up in a good dictionary. You will notice that, after the spelling of a word, its proper pronunciation is indicated by certain symbols for the vowels and consonants. At the bottom of each page of text of the better dictionaries is listed the key or interpretation of these signs. Become familiar with them, but there is no need to learn the list by heart. Frequent use will fix the various marks in your memory. Also glance through the "Guide to Pronunciation" and "The Rules for Syllabication" usually found in the introductory matter. Learn how to use this information when necessary.

All right, you've checked the words. Did you leave out a syllable? Did you add one? Did you fail to say *r* in *surprise?* Did you put the *l* before the *v* in *cavalry?* If you made any of these mistakes, you committed one of a number of common spoken errors that often become spelling errors.

The problem breaks down into four types of mispronunciation.

A. Extra Syllable

Some letter combinations in our language are difficult to produce orally. An *m* following an *l* is an example. The open mouth position must immediately be followed by closed lips, and stopped short. The tendency, therefore, is to add a syllable between the two letters to try to bridge the gap. Thus, we get *fillum* instead of *film.*

You can train yourself to speak correctly. Slow down your speech. Give each sound its full value before producing another. If you are in doubt about a word, or you hear other people saying it differently, look it up. Practice before a mirror. Watch your lip and jaw movements. Say it right, and you will spell it right!

SAY AND SPELL:

ATHLete	disas**TR**ous	remem**BR**ance
laun**DR**y	hin**DR**ance	barba**ROUS**
um**BR**ella	mischie**VOUS**	drow**NED**
	attac**KED**	

B. Omitted Syllable

It is just as wrong, of course, to leave out a syllable. Here the trouble arises out of speech that is too hurried. Slow up. Take it easy. Say the whole word. Don't say and write *joolery* instead of *jewelry*.

SAY AND SPELL:

act**UAL**ly	po**EM**	temp**ER**ature
prob**AB**ly	cho**CO**late	lab**OR**atory

C. Incorrect and Omitted Sounds

You may occasionally use the proper number of syllables in a word, but pronounce a particular letter incorrectly or leave it out altogether. You must not be careless. Get the dictionary habit. Don't say and spell *supprise* when you mean *surprise*.

SAY AND SPELL:

ar**C**tic	di**PH**theria	gover**N**ment
Feb**R**uary	sacril**E**gious	ques**TION**

D. Reversed Sounds

Usually this error occurs as the result of hearing the word spoken incorrectly and copying the mispronunciation without bothering to check. In this way, the little boy listens to his friend describe the charge of the "calvary," and may imitate this form for years before discovering that the word is *cavalry*. And imagine his dismay when he learns that there really is a word *calvary*, the hill where Christ was crucified!

SAY AND SPELL:

irrELEvant	trAGEdy
PERform	PERspiration

Right here there must be a question in your mind.

"What if I can say the word correctly, but still have trouble spelling it?"

That's fair enough. But don't forget the first three techniques. When you have removed the speech problem, treat the word like any other. **SEE IT, THINK IT, FEEL IT!** It's the basic attack. What we're doing now is giving you hints that can be applied to groups of words. However, the *see-think-feel* method is the guaranteed way, even if no other suggestion helps.

*   *   *

Now come additional problems related to speech.

E. The Indefinite Vowel

You know what a vowel is—a, e, i, o, u, or y (as in many and mystery). Because of the different sounds each of these can be—for example, *a* as in b*a*y, b*a*t, b*a*ll, b*a*r, bare—the pronunciation does not always tell us what the proper letter is. This is especially true in words where the middle vowel sound is little more than a grunt. In *relative*, merely pronouncing the word does not clearly tell us that an *a* should follow the *l*.

Suppose, however, whenever you have to spell *relative* you also think of *relate* (here the *a* is sharply marked). Then *relative* becomes easy. You can use this technique with many words that fall into this class—words in which the middle vowel sound is not clear, but where it *is* clear in a word from the same family.

Note these:

	Word	First Cousin
A	narrative	narrate
	sedative	sedate
	miracle	miraculous
E	arithmetic	arithmetical
	competition	compete
	celebration	celebrity
I	definite	define
	compilation	compile
	hypocrisy	hypocritical
O	frivolous	frivolity
	revolution	revolt
	consolation	console
U	exultation	exult
	sulphur	sulphuric
	future	futurity

*   *   *

You have probably had your troubles with the next group of speech-spelling puzzlers. These are words that come in pairs, or even appear as threesomes; they are pronounced exactly alike, or very nearly so, but have essential differences in meaning and spelling. You want to talk about a *stationary* object. You know that there is one word that uses an *a* and another that uses an *e* in the final syllables.

To handle these, we go back to the **THINK THE WORD** method. Create a bond between the difficult part and some bit of nonsense. Treat each word as if it were a separate unit and you will avoid confusion.

F. Think the Words That Sound Alike!

Look at these:

1. StationAry objects stAnd still.
   StationEry is used for lEttErs.

2. A princiPAL should be a PAL.
   The principAl idea is the mAin one.
   GrapPLE a princiPLE to your heart.

3. I can't EAT in hot wEATher.
   I don't know WHETher pie will WHET my appetite.

4. A grOAN is a loud mOAN.
   When I am grOWN I shall OWN a store.

5. I hEAR with my EAR.
   We looked hERE, thERE, everywhERE.

Some words are not even pronounced alike but are close enough to be troublesome.

Watch out for:

accept-except	prophecy-prophesy
affect-effect	moral-morale
angel-angle	canvas-canvass
council-counsel	loose-lose
quiet-quite	desert-dessert

Sometimes, in an effort to be informal or conversational, a speaker or writer will use contractions. These are single words that have been made out of two. For exemple, *it is* becomes *it's* in the contracted form. We have, in effect, substituted an apostrophe (') for the letter *i* between the *t* and the *s* and made one word. Do not confuse this with *its*, the form that does not use the *apostrophe* and that indicates possession. Whenever you are in doubt about *its* or *it's*, try the sentence, using the two words *it is*. If they fit, *it's* is correct; if they do not, use *its*.

Put this book in *it's* or *its* place.

Substitute *it is*. Does it make sense? It doesn't, of course. Use *its* in *its* place.

Note: There is no such form as *its'*.

This test also applies to *your* and *you're; who's* and *whose;* and *their, there,* and *they're.*

Here are some examples:

Your or *you're* not wanted here.
(Try *you are*. It fits. Therefore, use *you're*.)

Your or *you're* name is John.
(Try *you are*. It doesn't fit. Use *your*.)

I wonder *who's* or *whose* the winner.
(Try *who is*. It fits. Therefore, use *who's*.)

I know *who's* or *whose* hat that is.
(Try *who is*. It doesn't fit. Use *whose*.)

Their or *there* or *they're* coming Sunday.
(Try *they are*. It fits. Therefore, use *they're*.)

Their or *there* or *they're* is the place we stayed last year.
(Try *they are*. It doesn't fit. Use *there*. Indicates place.)

Their or *there* or *they're* team won.
(Try *they are*. It doesn't fit. Use *their*. Indicates possession.)

Remember:

It's *should've* or *should have*
—but never *should of!*

*　　　*　　　*

You've tried spelling rules before. You probably gave up in disgust, too. There were so many exceptions that you finished by being more harmed than helped. That's why we're going to bother with only those rules that work so often and with so many words that exceptions are of little consequence.

This brings us to the most valuable spelling rule in the language. It, too, is tied in with pronunciation. We'll review certain speech principles first, and afterward show how they apply in spelling to a vast number of words.

G. Accented Syllable Rule—when to double final consonants)

Vowels—We've talked about these before: *a, e, i, o, u,* and sometimes *y.*

Consonants—All the other letters in the alphabet. Observe that the *u* in *equip* has the effect of a *w.* When *u* is pronounced *w,* it is properly considered a consonant.

Accent—A syllable is that part of a word that is said all at once, without a break or pause in the rhythm. It might be compared to a musical note. We say the word *stop* in one continuous sound, and it would be represented in music by one note. Its technical name is *monosyllable* (*mono*—from the Greek, meaning one). *Polysyllables* (*poly*—many) are words that contain two or more syllables or pauses. In music, we would need two notes to represent *remit* (two syllables—*re-mit*) and three for *preference* (three syllables—*pre-fer-ence*). When we pronounce a single-syllable word (monosyllable), we place the same amount of stress on the whole word. However, in polysyllables, only one of the syllables receives the stress. When we pronounce polysyllabic words, we use added volume, or loudness, on the syllable that custom has dictated should receive what we call the accent.

reMIT—Added volume, or loudness, is placed on the second syllable.

LAbel—The first syllable receives the greater stress or accent.

PREFerence—Here again, the first syllable is accented. Note, however, how there is an accent shift to the second syllable in preFER, even though *preference* and *prefer* are in the same word family.

Spellick #3

Suppose you have used a dictionary to determine which syllable of a word should receive the accent. Yet when you say the word, you are not sure whether or not you have stressed the proper syllable. Try this device. Tear off a strip of paper about one half inch wide and two or three inches long. Now hold the strip of paper before your mouth as you pronounce a word of more than one syllable. As you speak, you will notice that the strip of paper will be blown forward at the precise moment that you stress the syllable that should be accented. If the paper has moved forward on the wrong syllable, practice until you get it right. At first, deliberately overdo the stressing sound, expelling the breath forcefully, so that you will have no difficulty recognizing the syllable at which you increased the volume.

*   *   *

We are now ready for the accented syllable rule, the most valuable of all spelling rules.

Observe these two groups of words:

DIF fer	oc **CUR**
LA bel	ad **MIT**
ED it	ex **PEL**

Similarities:

1. Each word ends in a *single consonant*.
2. Each final *single consonant* is preceded by a *single vowel*.

Major Differences:

1. In the group on the right, the accent falls on the *last syllable*.
2. In the group on the left, the accent falls on the *first syllable*.

Rule:

If a word ends in **one consonant** preceded by a **single vowel**,

If the syllable in which this combination appears is **accented**,

Double the final consonant before **adding a syllable beginning with a vowel.**

*   *   *

If the syllable in which the combination appears is **not accented, do not double** before adding a syllable beginning with a vowel.

We can condense the rule into a formula:

FSA *equals* **DOUBLE!**

F—final single consonant
S—single vowel preceding
A—accent on the combination

Let's put the **FSA** rule into practice. From the groups used as examples above, take the word *occur*. It ends in an *r* (single final consonant), the *r* is preceded by *u* (single vowel), and the stress falls on *cur* (accent on the combination).

Therefore:

ocCUR *plus* **ED** (syllable beginning with a vowel) *equals* occuRRed (doubled final consonant)

or
ocCUR *plus* **ENCE** *equals* occuRRence

or
ocCUR *plus* **ING** *equals* occuRRing

However:

Take the word *differ* from the column on the left. There is the final consonant *r*, and there is the single vowel *e*, but the stress falls on *dif*—which is *not the syllable containing the combination!*

Therefore:

DIFfer *plus* **ED** *equals* diffeRed
DIFfer *plus* **ENCE** *equals* diffeRence
DIFfer *plus* **ING** *equals* diffeRing

The consonant is not doubled because the accent does not fall on the syllable containing the single final consonant preceded by a single vowel.

Here's what happens to the rest of the words in the columns.

Last Syllable Not Accented	Last Syllable Accented
LAbel, labeLed, labeLing	adMIT, admiTTed,
EDit, ediTed, ediTing	admiTTance
	exPEL, expeLLed,
	expeLLing

In single syllable words, you don't have to worry about the accent because the stress automatically falls on the entire word. All you do is decide whether or not there is a single final consonant preceded by a single vowel.

stop, stoPPing, stoPPed
bat, baTTing, baTTed
flat, flaTTer, flaTTen

But:

meet, meeTing (two vowels precede the final consonant)

We have talked about accent shifts previously. Notice what happens to the word *prefer* when the stress changes from one syllable to another.

preFER, prefeRRed, prefeRRing

And:

PREFeRence (accent shifted to first syllable, no doubling)

Exceptions? Yes, there are some:

Double L's Instead of Single:

canceLLation	crystaLLize
chanceLLor	exceLLent

French Endings:

crocheTed   ricocheTed
(Note: Both words end in the *ay* sound, so that it is actually a vowel ending.)

Double Words:

overlaPPed   outfiTTed
(Note: The first consists of *over* and *lap* and has almost a double accent; therefore, this and others like it are treated as if the second half determines the spelling.)

Unreasonable Ones:

chagriNed   gaSeous
(That's right; there seems to be no reason why the single letters are used, but there they are!)

*   *   *

Suggestion:

If you want to remember the exceptions, set up **BONDS** for them; then **SEE** and **FEEL** them:

1. The chanCELLor gave an exCELLent reason for his canCELLation of the talk on the plant **CELL**.
2. CrocheTed and ricocheTed suit me to a **T**.
3. He overlaPPed his authority and overstePPed his bounds.
4. I had to **GRIN** when he was chaGRINed.
5. GASeous is the adjective of **GAS**.

Suggestion:

Ordinarily, rules with many exceptions are worthless. That's why such rules have been left out of this book. Certainly, it's easier to use the **SEE-THINK-FEEL** method. However, the **ACCENTED SYLLABLE** rule works with so many hundreds of words that it's one you ought to make a real effort to learn. Give it a try.

FSA *equals* **DOUBLE CONSONANT** (before added syllable beginning with a vowel).

Now practice with these:

Word	Add: ED	Word	Add: ING
comMIT	_____	beGIN	_____
conTROL	_____	reFER	_____
Open	_____	LEVel	_____
CAter	_____	OFfer	_____

Word	Add: ER	Word	Add: ANCE
REVel	_____	adMIT	_____
FAT	_____	reMIT	_____

Word	Add: OR	Word	Add: ENCE
BET	_____	conFER	_____
			(Watch shift!)
EDit	_____	inFER	_____

Answers: committed, controlled, opened, catered, beginning, referring, leveling, offering, reveler, fatter, admittance, remittance, bettor, editor, conference, inference.

Now the review paragraphs. Don't try them until you have studied the material in this chapter carefully. One look is not enough. Only when you are sure of each section are you ready to test yourself. The letter before each paragraph refers to the section where the words originally appeared in this chapter.

Diagnostic Paragraphs

A. Before going for his **laundry,** the **athlete** decided to attend a recent **film** that told the story of how **barbarous** tribes had once **attacked** the ancient Romans in the **disastrous** period of their decline. As he watched the picture, a **mischievous** little girl kept poking him with an **umbrella.** This proved quite a **hindrance** to his efforts to follow the scenes of **drowned** soldiers and burning houses. In his **remembrance,** he could not recall when he had been more annoyed.

B. Dr. Jones **actually** dropped the box of **chocolates** on his way home from the **laboratory.** However, he still had the **jewelry** for his wife, along with the birthday **poem,** so he knew her **temperature probably** wouldn't rise.

_____

_____

_____

C. Because of the **arctic** blasts common in **February,** it is no **surprise** that people recovering from **diphtheria** are told by doctors to stay indoors. In answer to a **question,** a **government** health agency agreed that this was wise. It would be almost **sacrilegious** to ignore both official and medical advice.

D. It is not **irrelevant** at this time to say that the **cavalry** has limited use today. The men who ride to war on horseback, however, do **perform** important jobs in hilly areas. Sending a tank up a steep pass would be inviting **tragedy.** With a little **perspiration,** mounted troops overcome such obstacles.

E. School had begun to act like a **sedative** on Bob. Preparing **sulphur** in his chemistry class, struggling with **arithmetic** problems, or reading how the **hypocrisy** of certain kings had led to **revolution** no longer interested him. He prayed for an academic **miracle** that would make the **compilation** of facts a **frivolous** task and destroy the **competition** for marks that brought **exultation** only to the brighter students. There was **consolation** in the **future,** however. A **relative** had sent Bob an invitation to spend the summer on a ranch. He eagerly glanced over his uncle's **narrative** of what they would do out West. Now he could look forward to a **definite celebration** from school work.

F. The **weather** was almost perfect. **Here** and **there** slivers of sunlight shot through the **stationary** branches like silver darts. **Everywhere** I could **hear** birds calling to one another. **There** was also the croaking of frogs to add a bass section to the **principal** theme of the forest concert. I wondered **whether** or not I should waste my time scrawling words on the **stationery** that lay in my lap. Then I thought of George's last letter:

"**It's** clear that **you're** like most people without **principle whose** main job seems to be to **groan** about **their** failure to write. **They're** expert at telling what they **should've** done, but **who's** to say why they didn't. This is **your** last chance, you should be **grown.** No reply this time and you'd better forget my address and **its** owner!"

I put pen to paper. Nature would have to wait.

G. The **editor opened** the **conference** by **leveling** a charge. Someone had **committed** the crime of **offering** a **bettor** a chance to make his profits **fatter** by showing him **preference** to **controlled** information. In fact, the meeting had been called by Mr. Grimes to mark the

_____

_____

_____

_____

beginning of his campaign for **stopping** the release of news as it **occurred** and before it was **edited.**

"You can draw your own **inference,**" he said. "I haven't **labeled** anyone, but it makes no **difference** to me who has **catered** to dishonest men. Whether or not he has received a **remittance** for his help, he will be **expelled,** and will never gain **admittance** to this office again. I'm **referring** to all when I say I would just as soon hire a drunken **reveler** as allow one of you to **flatten** the reputation of this paper. You've **batted** out of turn if you think I'm fooling."

_____

_____

The usual reminder:

Add the words you have missed in the diagnostic paragraph dictation to your personal list of words that need "The Treatment" *after* you have covered the first seven chapters.

SEE THE WORD!
THINK THE WORD!
FEEL THE WORD!
SAY THE WORD!
and finally . . .

· VI ·

Build the Word!

Most words are like pieces of clay. They can be com-
bined with other words to form larger pieces, or they can
be manipulated into a variety of shapes, depending upon
their use in a sentence. In the following paragraph, you
will find thirteen different forms and shades of meaning
derived from a single basic word, *love:*

Love is not alone for the **lovely. Loveliness** of heart
can **lovelier** be by far than of face, ofttimes **loved** briefly, but soon **loveless** and **lovelorn**—the **loveknot** broken,
the **lovebird** flown, and the **lovers** parted. Then no **loving**
hands will help the **lovesick** curl **lovable** hair into **lovelock** long.

This amorous adventure into word study brings us to
the relationship between grammar and spelling. Writing a
word correctly is sometimes only the beginning. It proves
you know one form. However, you must learn all the other
forms before you really have the situation, and your spelling, well in hand. You must become acquainted with a
word's whole family tree, its combining forms (*loveknot,
lovebird, lovelock*) as well as what are technically known
as its *parts of speech.* Let's briefly review the various func-
tions a word can perform in a sentence.

A. The Noun

This is the main thing we talk about in a sentence:
The *chair* is quite new.

or is part of a short group of words, called a *phrase:*
We walked (into the *woods*).
or may come at the end to help finish the thought:
I lifted the *box*.
or may appear in all three places at once:
The *launching* of the *ship* pleased the *town*.

Fundamentally, it is a name of:
1. **A Person**—*John* is my *brother*.
2. **A Place**—My *home* is in *New York*.
3. **A Thing**—A *shoe* is packed in a *box*.
4. **An Idea**—*Peace* feeds on *justice* and *understanding*.
5. **An Activity**—*Golf* is a good *sport*.

In brief, if it is a word that identifies anything you can see, hear, feel, taste, smell, or think about, it is a noun.

B. The Pronoun

Doesn't the following sound silly?

Mr. Mall rose from Mr. Mall's chair to get Mr. Mall's evening paper. Mr. Mall usually had it brought to Mr. Mall, but Mr. Mall had sent Mr. Mall's family on a visit to Mr. Mall's brother.

This sounds better:

Mr. Mall rose from *his* chair to get *his* evening paper. *He* usually had it brought to *him*, but *he* had sent *his* family on a visit to *his* brother.

The improvement was brought about by the use of *pronouns* or their adjectival forms. *"Pro"* comes from the Latin and means "instead of," or "for." Thus, pronouns are used instead of nouns. There are three kinds of pronouns.

1. **Personal**—used instead of readily identified names.

    I, me, we, us (first person)
    mine, ours (first person possessive)

    you (second person)
    yours (second person possessive)

    he, him, she, her, they, them (third person)
    his, hers, theirs (third person possessive)

    my, our, your, his, her, their (adjective forms)

    Example: See paragraph about Mr. Mall.

2. **Indefinite**—as the term suggests, used when no one in particular is meant, but one person at a time is being considered.
    each, either, neither, one
    somebody, everybody, nobody, anybody
    someone, everyone, no one, anyone

    Example: *Everybody* is eating his lunch.

3. **Relative**—used to refer to people or things **and to** connect one part of a sentence to another.

(for people) *who, whoever, whosoever, whom, whomever, whomsoever*

(for things) *which*

(for either) *that*

Examples: Tom is the one *whom* I called. (or *that*)
The suit *which* I want is expensive. (or *that*)

C. The Verb

The verb indicates what and when a noun or pronoun did something:

> The **lion** *roared* madly.

(Tells us what the lion—*noun*—did—at a previous date.)

or just makes a statement:

> We *are* very tired.

(Enables us to make a statement about "We"—*pronoun*—at this moment.)

The verb may consist of *one word*, as above:

> **or two:** I *have eaten* already.
> **or three:** They *have been traveling*.
> **or four:** By this time Sunday, I *shall have been fishing* for two hours.

The verb sometimes changes when the number changes:

> **Singular** (*one person, place, or thing,* etc.): George *walks* to work.
> **Plural** (*2 or more people, places, or things,* etc.): They *walk* every day.

The verb also has tense, or indicates time:

Tomorrow (*future*): *shall* or *will paint, have painted, have been painting.*
Today (*present*): *paints, paint, am, is, are painting.*
Yesterday (*past*): *painted, was, were painting, has, have, had painted, has, have, had been painting.*

D. The Adjective

If we had only the names for objects and people, our language would be dull and lack color and emotion. The *adjective* helps us get a better picture of a *noun or pronoun*. It may be directly attached to a word and influence its meaning:

I want a *large* piece of cake.
   (causes quantity to defeat manners)

She invited *only* me.
   (makes one exclusive)

or be separated from the word it influences by a verb:

That boy is *noisy.*
   (helps to warn one in advance)

The adjective may **merely describe:** *tall* man
or compare (**comparative degree**): *taller* than I
or select from three or more (**superlative degree**): *tallest* of the group

E. The Adverb

Most frequently, the *adverb* gives us more information about a *verb*. That's why the "ad" syllable, meaning "toward, to," plus the "verb" is a very good definition in itself. Sometimes, however, the adverb may also describe an adjective or another adverb. Here are three examples:

1. Please tell the story *quickly*. ("tell" how?—information about a verb)
2. This table is *unusually* heavy. (how "heavy"?—information about an adjective)
3. She replied *rather* angrily. (how "angrily"?—information about an adverb)

The adverb may also **merely describe:** *slowly*
or compare: *more slowly*
or select from three or more: *most slowly*

* * *

There are other parts of speech, and books have been written on the principles of grammar that we have chosen *not* to discuss. But remember: We are interested in the subject only where it helps our spelling.

Certain helpful rules can be applied to words as they change from one part of speech to another. Study these rules carefully. Use them as further aids: Each shows how to **BUILD THE WORD!**

1. The "Y" Ending

When *y* is preceded by a consonant, *change y to i!*

a. Nouns: When the plural is formed—

country, countries   *pantry, pantries*
city, cities   *baby, babies*

b. Verbs: When the tense changes—

try, tries, tried—BUT—*trying* (to avoid double *i*)
cry, cries, cried—BUT—*crying* (to avoid double *i*)
comply, complies, complied—BUT—*complying* (to avoid double *i*)
reply, replies, replied—BUT—*replying* (to avoid double *i*)

c. Adjectives: When making comparisons—

hearty, heartier, heartiest
lazy, lazier, laziest
cozy, cozier, coziest
busy, busier, busiest (also noun: *business*)

d. Adverbs: When formed from adjectives—

hearty, heartily   *cozy, cozily*
lazy, lazily   *busy, busily*

When *y* is preceded by a vowel (*a, e, i, o, u*), *keep the y!*

a. Nouns: When the plural is formed—

monkey, monkeys   *donkey, donkeys*
key, keys   *alloy, alloys*

b. **Verbs: When the tense changes—**

play, played, am playing, plays
survey, surveyed, was surveyed, surveys
lay, are laying, lays—BUT—*laid, lain*
slay, was slaying, slays—BUT—*slain*

c. **Adjectives and Adverbs:**

coy, coyly   *boy, boyish, boyishly*
cloy, cloying, cloyingly

d. **Two important exceptions:**

day, daily   *gay, gaily*

2. The Silent "E" Ending

Many words in the language end in *e*. Frequently, as in *tape, supreme, kite, rope,* and *use,* the letter is there to retain the "long" sound of the preceding vowel. At other times, there does not seem to be any good reason for its presence, as in *salve, prove, suit,* and *love,* but it is there just the same. Because it only helps the sound of another letter, or is a useless remnant, it is called the **silent vowel.** When syllables are added to words ending in this silent *e* to change them into other parts of speech, special rules apply.

Example:
    tribe (silent *e*)
    al (syllable beginning with a vowel)
    tribal (*The silent e is dropped when a syllable beginning with a vowel is added.*)

Example:

> grieve
> ance
> grievance *(The silent e is dropped.)*

Try these:

Word	Add	
skate	ing	_____
blue	ish	_____
advise	ing	_____
	able	_____
use	able	_____
	age	_____
	ing	_____
console	ation	_____

Answers: skating, bluish, advising, advisable, usable, usage, using, consolation.

There are a few exceptions, but they are logical, so that you should remember them easily. If you have any trouble, fall back on the **SEE-THINK-FEEL THE WORD** treatment.

a. *canoeing, hoeing*—to avoid pronunciation difficulty, the *e* is retained. (also: *shoe, toe*)

b. *dyeing, singeing*—to avoid confusing them with *dying, singing,* the *e* is retained. (also: *tinge*)

c. *ce* and *ge* endings—to retain the sound of *s* in *ce,* and *dj* in *ge,* the *e* is kept in the word. (*serviceable, manageable, changeable, advantageous, courageous*)

d. *mileage*—to avoid confusing it with *millage* (tax rate in mills per dollar) and to retain the long *i* sound, the *e* is kept.

The other part of this rule is not so reliable. When the silent *e* is followed by a syllable beginning with a consonant, the practice *generally* is to retain the *e*, as in *grateful, lately, lameness, abatement.* There are numerous exceptions, however, and you are advised to check the individual words with a dictionary rather than depend on the rule. Watch out particularly for *argument, judgment,* and *acknowledgment.* And make sure you spell *sincerely* and *nineteen* correctly; they *do* follow the rule. Lastly, *development* has nothing to do with the rule at all because the original word is *develop* (no silent *e* ending)!

3. The "LY" Ending

The most frequent use of the *ly* syllable is to change adjectives into adverbs. When you are in doubt about the spelling of a word ending in *ly:*

a. Write the adjective form first.

b. Check the last letter.

If it is *y*, treat it like any *y* ending.

necessary	*y* to *i*	*necessarily*
heavy	*y* to *i*	*heavily*

If it is *le,* change *e* to *y,* and that's all!

considerable	*e* to *y*	*considerably*
capable	*e* to *y*	*capably*

If it is *l,* leave it there!

usual	*l* stays	*usually*
oral	*l* stays	*orally*

If it is *e,* leave it there!

extreme	*e* stays	*extremely*
late	*e* stays	*lately*

Add *ly* to these:

satisfactory	_____	definite	_____
merry	_____	absolute	_____
happy	_____	sincere	_____
personal	_____	able	_____
natural	_____	double	_____
awful	_____	subtle	_____

Answers: satisfactorily, merrily, happily, personally, naturally, awfully, definitely, absolutely, sincerely, ably, doubly, subtly.

4. The "ABLE–IBLE" Endings

Unfortunately, this rule is somewhat unreliable. The only reason it is included here is that you may need to make an informed guess at a time when a dictionary is not available. I use the word _guess_ advisedly because of the exceptions. But in a pinch, try the following guides, which will work most of the time. However, as soon as you can, check with a dictionary to see whether or not you have guessed right! If you haven't, add the word(s) to your personal list for further treatment.

a. Use _able_ if—

a whole word is left after you drop the last syllable:

depend	_dependable_
commend	_commendable_
tax	_taxable_
profit	_profitable_
prefer	_preferable_

a whole word would have been left if you had not dropped the silent _e:_

use	usable
receive	receivable
advise	advisable
compare	comparable
desire	desirable

the root word ends in a *y* that was changed to *i* before the added syllable:

envy	enviable
justify	justifiable
rely	reliable
deny	deniable
pity	pitiable

a related word ends in *ate* or *ation:*

duration	durable
placate	implacable
irritate	irritable
tolerate	tolerable
inflation	inflatable

b. Use *ible* if—

you do not have a whole word left after you drop the last syllable:

aud	audible
feas	feasible
neglig	negligible
terr	terrible
plaus	plausible

(Lots of exceptions here: *affable, amenable, capa-*

ble, formidable, inevitable, inexorable, inscrutable, vulnerable, etc.)

you have a complete word left *but* can form another word ending in *ion:*

access	*accession*	*accessible*
collect	*collection*	*collectible*
deduct	*deduction*	*deductible*
digest	*digestion*	*digestible*
corrupt	*corruption*	*corruptible*

the root word has an *ive* or *ion* ending in one of its forms:

permit	*permission*	*permissible*
divide	*divisive*	*divisible*
resist	*resistive*	*resistible*
revert	*reversion*	*reversible*
convert	*conversion*	*convertible*

the root of the word, after you drop the final syllable, ends in the sound of *c* (as in force) or the sound of *g* (as in forge):

forc	*forcible*
reduc	*reducible*
elig	*eligible*
intang	*intangible*
illeg	*illegible*

c. Watch for these:

remittable (but *remissible*)
collapsible	*contemptible*
discernible	*gullible*

5. The "C" Ending

Notice these two examples:

colic, colicky   *picnic, picnicked, picnicking*

The *k* is added before the final syllable to prevent sounding the *c* like an *s.*

Try it with these:

shellac, panic, traffic
(Add *ing, ed, er,* or *y,* if possible)

Answers: shellacking, shellacked, panicked, panicky, trafficking, trafficked.

6. The "EFY–IFY" Ending

Only four words that you are likely to use end in *efy:*

liquefy	*stupefy*
rarefy	*putrefy*

Use *ify* with others like:

pacify	*purify*	*qualify*
testify	*classify*	*petrify*
fortify	*rectify*	*codify*

7. The "FULL" Ending

In general, when you add this syllable to a word, omit one of the *l's.*

hope, hopeful   *skill, skillful, skilful*
spite, spiteful   *fate, fateful*

8. The "SEDE, CEED, CEDE" Endings

a. Only one word in the language uses S:
superSede

b. Three words use CEED:
proCEED, sucCEED, exCEED

c. All others use CEDE:

reCEDE   preCEDE
conCEDE   interCEDE, and so on

9. Unusual Plural Endings

a. "O"

If the singular form ends in an *o* preceded by a consonant, usually add *es*.

echo, echoes   *potato, potatoes*
Negro, Negroes   *cargo, cargoes*

If the singular form ends in an *o* preceded by a vowel, always add only *s*.

cameo, cameos   *patio, patios*
studio, studios   *ratio, ratios*

Also:

musical terms—*altos, sopranos*

clipped words—*photos, autos*
recent words—*gauchos, commandos*

b. "Y"

We have already covered this:

Y preceded by a consonant, change *y* to *i*, and add *es*.
Y preceded by a vowel, add only *s*.

puppy, puppies	*relay, relays*
berry, berries	*convoy, convoys*

c. Irregular Nouns

Words taken from a foreign language often present problems. No general rules exist, so that each one must be checked with a dictionary. The best approach here, too, is the SEE-THINK-FEEL treatment.

hippopotamus, hippopotamuses, hippopotami
alumnus, alumni (male), alumna, alumnae
   (female)
phenomenon, phenomena

10. Front Syllables

So far we have been talking about spelling problems that are created by the addition of syllables at the ends of words. Many errors occur also at the beginnings, especially when the question of doubling a letter arises. You can handle these without trouble if you use this method:

a. Single Letter

disappear

A common misspelling of this word is to use an extra *s*. Here's what to do:

Separate the first syllable from the basic word:

> *dis appear*

What does it end with? *s.*
What does the rest begin with? *a.*
Any double letter? *No!*

Again:

> *dis appoint   disappoint*

Ends-*s*   Begins-*a*   Double? *No!*

b. Double Letter

> *misspell*

Separate the first syllable from the basic word:

> *mis spell*

What does it end with? *s.*
What does the rest begin with? *s.*
Any double letter? *Yes!* Double *s.*

Again:

> *dis service   disservice*

Ends-*s*   Begins-*s*   Double? *Yes!*

A few more of both kinds:

un necessary	*unnecessary*
re commend	*recommend*
dis approve	*disapprove*
a cross	*across*
ad dress	*address*

11. Hyphenated Expressions

The tendency today is to use the hyphen (-) as little as possible. In fact, experts who prefer its use have been unable to agree on a set of rules. Therefore, when you aren't sure, leave out the hyphen. These are the preferred uses about which there is general agreement.

a. Fused adjectives, numbers

   i. Several words combined to form one adjective:

      never-to-be-forgotten day
      well-executed double play

   ii. *Twenty-one, thirty-three,* and so on, up to *ninety-nine*

b. "ex" and "self":

When these syllables are attached to the beginning of a word, use the hyphen.

     ex-private   *self-appointed*   *ex-counterman*

c. Before a capital letter or a similar vowel

    un-American   *re-echo*
    pro-British   *co-owner*

12. The Apostrophe (')

This symbol is used in a variety of situations. If you omit a necessary apostrophe, you have misspelled the word, even though the error did not involve a letter.

a. To indicate possession, ownership:

This is its major use. Here, too, there is a lack of agreement among the experts. Fortunately, the easiest rule to apply also happens to be the most modern.

i. If the word ends in *s*, use only (').

Boys play games. I enjoy watching *boys'* games.
Charles had a hat. Who took *Charles'* hat?
Have you read *Dickens' A Tale of Two Cities?*

ii. If the word does **not end in** *s*, use (*'s*).

These are *children's* toys.
We looked for the *girl's* blue coat.
Ladies will exercise a *lady's* privilege.

iii. In groups of two or more, the last number receives the mark.

It's occupied by *Chisholm and Boone's* law firm.
I'm tired of every *Tom, Dick, and Harry's* complaint.

iv. In hyphenated expressions, place the mark at the end.

She visited her *son-in-law's* house.
Ask the *sergeant-at-arms'* permission.

v. Use mark on nouns or pronouns preceding words ending in "ing." (No mark for personal pronouns.)

They discussed *Cole's* leaving the force.
I wondered whether or not someone *else's* winning would upset her.
They didn't approve of *my* going.

Important! Remember these personal pronouns **never use the apostrophe!**

mine, ours	*yours*
his, hers, its	*theirs*
whose	

b. Plurals of letters and numbers:

How many "*r's*" does the word have?
There are three *2's* in my number.
The company's president used too many "and's" in his speech.

c. Contractions:

See Chapter V, p. 35.

13. Capital Letters

Good spelling habits require that you use these carefully.

a. Titles of books, plays, articles, newspapers, magazines, and so on.

The first and last words of a title are always written

with capital letters. In the rest, only articles (*a, an, the*), prepositions (*of, by, to*), and conjunctions (*and, if, as*), when they are shorter than four letters, may be written without capitals.

> *The Taming of the Shrew*
> *The Shape of Things to Come*
> *What Men Live By*

b. Proper Nouns

Any word that becomes the name of a particular place, person, or thing should be capitalized. Very often, the same word may be either proper or common.

Observe:

> He bought a piece of *territory* in the *northwest* part of the state.
> The establishment of the *Northwest Territory* raised controversial issues.
> People who live in the *north* frequently go to the *south* in the winter.
> The Civil War involved the *North* against the *South.*

Note:

When a proper noun becomes an adjective, the capital letter is retained.

> *France* is the place to study *French* customs.
> If you plan to travel to South America, learn the *Spanish* language.

c. First Words

Lines of Poetry

"*Take* her up tenderly,
Lift her with care,
Fashioned so slenderly,
Young and so fair."

Direct Quotations

"*Off* with her head!" shouted Henry.
Henry shouted, "*Off* with her head!"

Salutations, Closings of Letters

Dear Mr. Smith:
Sincerely yours,

Rewrite the following, inserting all capital letters that have been left out:

> 72 ellen drive
> rockaway, new jersey
> january 6, 19—

dear john,
    when i spoke to you about "south pacific," i didn't realize that your french cousin had expressed a desire to go, too. well, as shakespeare said,
    "let me not to the marriage of true minds
    admit impediments"
    in this case, i'll be preacher jones, and perform the ceremony of wedding broadway to gallic charm.

> cordially,
> horton

Now check:

> 72 Ellen Drive
> Rockaway, New Jersey
> January 6, 19—

Dear John,

When I spoke to you about "South Pacific," I didn't realize that your French cousin had expressed a desire to go, too. Well, as Shakespeare said,

"Let me not to the marriage of true minds
Admit impediments"

In this case, I'll be Preacher Jones and perform the ceremony of wedding Broadway to Gallic charm.

> Cordially,
> Horton

The review paragraphs in this chapter will contain samplings rather than the complete list of words used as illustration. You understand, of course, that the main stress is on rules rather than on individual words. Your knowledge of these (and some exceptions) is what we want to test. If a rule doesn't seem to help with a particular word, give it "The Treatment" (see Chapter VII).

Diagnostic Paragraph

Special Endings

Willie almost **cried** when he came face to face with the **monkeys**. For some reason, they reminded him of furry **babies**, but the way they **lazily surveyed** him made him feel sure they were very old. Suddenly, Uncle Jasper invited Willie to go **canoeing**. It was a **commendable** suggestion meant to keep the boy **manageable**. However, it was going to be **extremely** difficult to start the trip **happily** because at the moment tears seemed **irresistible**.

Suddenly again, two astounding **phenomena interceded** in **panicky** Willie's behalf. First, a group of **sopranos,** sitting in a **convertible,** drove by, singing "Lonesome **Cargoes.**" Then, a **tribal** chieftain, wearing a string of **cameos, skillfully** began leading two **hippopotamuses** into a dance. So **advantageous** was this welcome change that Willie allowed a **grateful** grin to **supersede** his **boyishly** sad expression. Then Willie woke up. It had been a dreadful nightmare, enough to **stupefy** the mind.

Front Syllables, Hyphens, Apostrophes

What is meant by the term **"un-American"?** Well, **it's** many things. One who **disapproves** of **everyone's** right to speak freely is offering a **disservice** to his country. The **self-appointed** critic of **another's** beliefs acts **unpatriotically** when he **recommends** that even a **person's** thinking should be controlled. Abraham Lincoln, in several **addresses,** spoke of the need for **well-developed** citizens from **twenty-one** to **seventy-one** who would become **co-owners** of a country that accepted every **Tom, Dick,** and **Harry's** differences, allowed no **"anti's"** to develop against any group, and used the three **"r's"** to be watchful of your interests and **theirs.** In this way, fearing some **so-called** strong man would become **unnecessary. Unable** to make headway, such an individual would quickly learn that a **dictator's** hand could not reach **across** the land without **its** being broken.

_____

_____

_____

The last two chapters have thrown rules at you by the handful. Perhaps by now you wish you had skipped them. There are so many things to remember.

It isn't really that bad. Bear in mind that the majority of words cannot be classified. They require individual study. You know how to do that. If you prefer to use the **SEE-THINK-FEEL** method for all words, fine! Any rule that _bothers you_ isn't worth _bothering with_. If you can remember the rule easily, and it helps, use it. If you can't, forget the rule, and treat each word by itself.

The Treatment

Six Minutes A Day!

It's time to take stock. You now know the basic system that can be *applied to any word:*

SEE THE WORD!

> Get a picture in your mind, especially of the difficult part of the word.

THINK THE WORD!

> Prepare some bit of easily remembered nonsense for the troublesome syllable or letter.

FEEL THE WORD!

> Trace the word *with your finger,* and learn to write it while concentrating on something else.

You are also familiar with the devices for handling large groups of words:

SAY THE WORD!

> Be careful not to leave out, add, or confuse syllables and letters. Use other words in the same

family to locate key vowels in words. Be careful of words that sound alike. Learn the *accented syllable rule! FSA!*

BUILD THE WORD!

Follow the changes in spelling from one part of speech to another. Study unusual plurals, front and back syllables, hyphens, possessives, and capital letters.

These are the five steps we mentioned in the first chapter. Together they are the tested way to make the correct spelling of any word a lifelong habit. Now we are going to prescribe a simple *six-minute-a-day program* to make sure that good spelling stays with you forever. It explains how to give any word "The Treatment."

DAILY PROGRAM

Time	Procedure
Morning	A. Look up the pronunciation of your troublesome word in a good dictionary.
3 minutes	**SAY THE WORD.** Then observe how it is built.
	Set up the image to **SEE THE WORD.** Stare at it for ten seconds. Look away at another surface. Count five; "see" the image with your mind. Write the word rapidly. (90 seconds)

B. Prepare the *bond*.

THINK THE WORD.

Write the word as you think of the association. (30 seconds)

C. Write the word in large script letters.

FEEL THE WORD by tracing it three times with your finger.

Say each letter aloud as you trace.

Write the word rapidly, and as you do, say anything that comes into your mind, or repeat the association. (60 seconds)

Afternoon	Repeat the entire procedure outlined above, except for looking up the word in the dictionary.
1 minute, 30 seconds	This should take about half the time it took you in the morning because you are simply recalling what you have done.
	Do not skip any steps. It will require patience, but stay with it.
Evening	Repeat everything once more.
1 minute,	Don't try more than *one word a day.*
30 seconds	Anything more will divide your attention

and reduce the single effect you want to establish.

With this plan, you can cover five words from Monday to Friday. Use the weekend for review by preparing a few sentences or a paragraph that contains the words you studied that week. Ask someone to dictate the material, if possible, or record it.

In the next chapter, you will find a *thirty-day trial* that uses the six-minute-a-day routine. Before you go ahead, make certain you understand the step-by-step procedure that helps you give any word "The Treatment."

· VIII ·

Thirty-Day Trial

Once you are completely familiar with the basic system of how to give any word "The Treatment," you are ready to prove to yourself that good spellers are made, not born. What follows is a long-range practice session, a *thirty-day trial* broken down into weekly units featuring the word-a-day plan discussed in the previous chapter. The purpose here, of course, is to show you how to train yourself to attack your spelling problems systematically.

The diagnostic list for the thirty-day trial consists of sixty words (See *Appendix*, p. 203). These so-called demons are not particularly unusual or difficult, but they are commonly misspelled by more than 25 percent of educated people.

You may already know how to spell many of the words. To find out which words need further study, test yourself with the *diagnostic sentences* provided with the list, using the dictation or recording method. After you have tested yourself, select the first twenty words that you have misspelled. These will form your personal list for your trial session. Save others you have misspelled for another time.

To illustrate how you should set up your thirty-day trial, I have selected twenty words in the diagnostic list and have prepared a typical daily, weekly, and end-of-the-month unit. You might want to practice with the words used, whether or not you can spell them, just to get into the swing of the program. However, if you prefer, use your own list of twenty, and set them up according to the SAMPLE MONTHLY UNIT that follows *the eight important suggestions that will help you develop the proper practice habits:*

1. Take one word a day, and spend six minutes on it. Study each one exactly as outlined in the sample unit. Cover five words a week. Use Saturdays and Sundays for review. For the monthly review, prepare several paragraphs, again like those in the sample. The entire procedure should require about three hours, including two hours for the words and about an hour for the sentences and paragraphs. Is it worth spending three hours a month to become a perfect speller?

2. Before you proceed with a word, check its pronunciation in a dictionary, **even if you think you know it;** then write it in pencil in the space provided on each page of the sample unit. I have deliberately omitted this information, so that you will train yourself to use the dictionary often as the final authority on the spoken word.

3. Use the spaces under "Image" for additional diagrams you may think of, under "Bond" for further nonsense associations, and under "Trace" for writing the word in script during the daily review. **Your own handwriting** should form the basis for the tracing practice.

4. You will note that at the bottom of each day's exercises are three sentences, each using a different form of the word you have studied. This has been done so that you can see the importance of learning the whole "family tree" of a word. Use the fifteen sentences composed for the five words covered in the weekend reviews. Take ten (two for

each word) on Saturday and five (one for each word) on Sunday.

5. A notation like "VI—Front Syllables" refers to the rule or suggestion covered in the chapter indicated by the Roman numeral. Review the section as you practice.

6. If possible, form a team with another person working on spelling. Help each other by exchanging dictation of test paragraphs and sentences. Write weekly letters in which you purposely use newly learned words.

7. Do not assume that you need peace and quiet for your practice sessions. Train yourself to concentrate even in the midst of great noise and confusion. Make your spelling automatic!

8. Before you start, be sure you understand and can apply the techniques discussed in previous chapters. Also be certain you can follow the six-minute-a-day program. Once you do start, don't let yourself give up. Be serious. Be faithful. Six minutes each day. That's all.

And now, here is the SAMPLE MONTHLY UNIT for your thirty-day trial:

FIRST WEEK: Monday
Word 1:   co op er a tion

Pronunciation: _____

Image: COOPeration
  See A,
  page 74   _____

                 _____

Bond: I need your COOPeration to clean the
  See B,   COOP.
  page 75   See VI—Front Syllables

                 _____

                 _____

Trace: _____ *cooperation* _____
  See C,
  page 75   _____

Sentences: **Cooperation** among nations will lead
                 to peace.
                    We have been **cooperating** in the
                 drive.
                    It was good of you to **cooperate.**

FIRST WEEK: Tuesday
Word 2:   ac quaint ance

Pronunciation: _____

Image: acQUAINTAnce

                 _____

                 _____

Bond: My acquaintance speaks with a
                 QUAINT A.

                 _____

                 _____

Trace: *acquaintance*

                 _____

Sentences: My **acquaintance** is coming to see me.
                 We are becoming **acquainted** with
                 each other.
                 I shall wait while you are **acquainting**
                 her with the details.

FIRST WEEK: Wednesday

Word 3: gov ern ment

Pronunciation: _____

Image: goVERNment

_____

_____

Bond: VERN Porter works for the goV-ERNment.

See V—Omitted Syllables

_____

_____

Trace: *government*

_____

Sentences: **Government** separates men from beasts.

Only the **governable** avoid lawlessness.

Will you live up to your promises when you are **governor?**

FIRST WEEK: **Thursday**

Word 4:   re quire ment

Pronunciation: _____

Image: reQUIREment

               _____

               _____

Bond: A QUIRE of paper will meet my re-
QUIREment.
See VI—Silent "E" Ending

               _____

               _____

Trace: _requirement_

               _____

Sentences: One **requirement** is a local address.
What you **required** was not available.
He spoke of new shipments **requiring**
more space.

FIRST WEEK: Friday
Word 5:   ex cel lent

Pronunciation: _____

Image: exCELLEnt

_____

_____

Bond: The prisoner in CELL E shows ex-CELLEnt conduct.

_____

_____

Trace: *excellent*

_____

Sentences: **Excellent** apples can be bought now.
We know of her **excellence** in the dance.
To **excel** is to stand out.

FIRST WEEK REVIEW: 10 Sentences on Saturday

1. **Cooperation** among nations will lead to peace.
2. My **acquaintance** is coming to see me.
3. **Government** separates men from beasts.
4. One **requirement** is a local address.
5. **Excellent** apples can be bought now.
6. We have been **cooperating** in the drive.
7. We are becoming **acquainted** with each other.
8. Only the **governable** avoid lawlessness.
9. What you **required** was not available.
10. We know of her **excellence** in the dance.

5 Sentences on Sunday

1. It was good of you to **cooperate.**
2. I shall wait while you are **acquainting** her with the details.
3. Will you live up to your promises when you are **governor?**
4. He spoke of new shipments **requiring** more space.
5. To **excel** is to stand out.

SECOND WEEK: Monday

Word 6:   def i nite

Pronunciation: _____

Image: defInIte

                      _____

                      _____

Bond: An I for an I is a defInIte biblical
                      saying.

                      _____

                      _____

Trace: ___*definite*___

                      _____

Sentences: **Definite** signs of spring are here.
                      We are **definitely** going tomorrow.
                      How do you **define** the word?

SECOND WEEK: Tuesday
Word 7:   cas u al ty

Pronunciation: _____

Image: CASUALty

                   _____

                   _____

Bond: One cannot be CASUAL about a
               CASUALty.

                   _____

                   _____

Trace: *casualty*

                   _____

Sentences: The **casualty** figures mounted as the
               battle wore on.
                   Criminals are often **casualties** of pov-
               erty.
                   He dressed **casually** but well.

SECOND WEEK: Wednesday

Word 8: sense

Pronunciation: _____

Image: seNSe

_____

_____

Bond: NS means "no seNSe."

_____

_____

Trace: _____ *sense* _____

_____

Sentences: **Sense** comes with experience.
Why aren't you **sensible** about it?
She is much too **sensitive.**

SECOND WEEK: Thursday
Word 9:   bul le tin

Pronunciation: _____

Image: BULLET IN

                _____

                _____

Bond: The BULLET lodged IN the BULLE-
                TIN board.

                _____

                _____

Trace: *bulletin*

                _____

Sentences: **Bulletin** 9 will be issued on Monday.
                Bulletins were received every hour.
                The message will be **bulletined** every-
                where.

SECOND WEEK: Friday

Word 10:   oc ca sion

Pronunciation: _____

Image: oCCasion

                  _____

                  _____

Bond: A 2 CC dose will do for this oCCa-
                  sion.

                  _____

                  _____

Trace: *occasion*

                  _____

Sentences: An **occasion** like this will be long re-
                  membered.
                  We send each other **occasional** letters.
                  Try to relax **occasionally.**

SECOND WEEK REVIEW: 10 Sentences on Saturday

1. **Definite** signs of spring are here.
2. The **casualty** figures mounted as the battle wore on.
3. **Sense** comes with experience.
4. **Bulletin** 9 will be issued on Monday.
5. An **occasion** like this will be long remembered.
6. We are **definitely** going tomorrow.
7. Criminals are often **casualties** of poverty.
8. Why aren't you **sensible** about it?
9. **Bulletins** were received every hour.
10. We send each other **occasional** letters.

5 Sentences on Sunday

1. How do you **define** the word?
2. He dressed **casually** but well.
3. She is much too **sensitive.**
4. The message will be **bulletined** everywhere.
5. Try to relax **occasionally.**

THIRD WEEK: Monday

Word 11:   rec om men da tion

Pronunciation: _____

Image: reCoMMendation

_____

_____

Bond: I C the MM's in reCoMMendation.
                  See VI—Front Syllables

_____

_____

Trace: *recommendation*

_____

Sentences: **Recommendation** is essential for a
                  job.
                      We are **recommending** a new building.
                      Whether or not you are **recommend-
                  able** for the position is a question.

THIRD WEEK: Tuesday
Word 12:   fi nan cial

Pronunciation: _____

Image: fINANcial

                _____

                _____

Bond: FINANcial success begins IN AN account with a bank.

                _____

                _____

Trace: _financial_

                _____

Sentences: **Financial** news is found in most newspapers.

        They are **financially** reliable.

        The suspected **financier** left the country.

THIRD WEEK: Wednesday
Word 13:   de ter mine

Pronunciation: _____

Image: deterMINE

                  _____

                  _____

Bond: MINE will deterMINE the final result.

                  _____

Trace: _*determine*_

                  _____

Sentences: **Determine** the answer by dividing.
                  Make a **determined** effort.
                  George showed great **determination.**

THIRD WEEK: Thursday

Word 14:   nec es sar y

Pronunciation: _____

Image: neCESSary

_____

_____

Bond: It is neCESSary to keep a CESSpool clean.

_____

_____

Trace: _necessary_

_____

Sentences: **Necessary** steps are being taken.
Is that a **necessity?**
It isn't **necessarily** so.

THIRD WEEK: Friday

Word 15: quan ti ty

Pronunciation: _____

Image: quANTITY

_____

_____

Bond: A quANTITY of ants might be called an ANTITY.

_____

_____

Trace: *quantity*

_____

Sentences: **Quantity** is what we need now.
In what **quantities** do you want it?
The chemist made a **quantitative** analysis.

THIRD WEEK REVIEW: 10 Sentences on Saturday

1. **Recommendation** is essential for a job.
2. **Financial** news is found in most newspapers.
3. **Determine** the answer by dividing.
4. **Necessary** steps are being taken.
5. **Quantity** is what we need now.
6. We are **recommending** a new building.
7. They are **financially** reliable.
8. Make a **determined** effort.
9. Is that a **necessity**?
10. In what **quantities** do you want it?

5 Sentences on Sunday

1. Whether or not you are **recommendable** for the position is a question.
2. The suspected **financier** left the country.
3. George showed great **determination.**
4. It isn't **necessarily** so.
5. The chemist made a **quantitative** analysis.

FOURTH WEEK: Monday

Word 16: con science

Pronunciation: _____

Image: conSCIENCE

_____

_____

Bond: CON plus SCIENCE equals CON-SCIENCE.

_____

_____

Trace: *conscience*

_____

Sentences: **Conscience** makes cowards of us all.

If you are **conscientious,** you will succeed.

It was a **conscious** act of violence.

FOURTH WEEK: Tuesday
Word 17:   au thor i ty

Pronunciation: _____

Image: auTHORity

_____

_____

Bond: The god THOR was an ancient sym-
                bol of auTHORity.

_____

_____

Trace: *authority*

_____

Sentences: **Authority** should rest with the wise
                and just.
                I object to your **authoritarian** tone.
                We studied the **authoritative** docu-
                ment.

FOURTH WEEK: Wednesday
Word 18: · ben e fit

Pronunciation: _____

Image: BENEfit

_____

_____

Bond: The BENE in BENEfit means "well" in Latin.

_____

_____

Trace: *benefit*

_____

Sentences: **Benefit** yourself by checking the value.
The outcome proved to be **beneficial.**
Who has **benefited** from the loan?

FOURTH WEEK: Thursday

Word 19:   ba sis

Pronunciation: _____

Image: baSIS

_____

_____

Bond: Billy was punished on the baSIS of what SIS said.

_____

_____

Trace: _____ *basis* _____

_____

Sentences: The **basis** for his action was the report.

The **basic** idea was sound.

Their vote shows that they are **basically** opposed.

FOURTH WEEK: Friday

Word 20: ex ist ence

Pronunciation: _____

Image: exisTENce

_____

_____

Bond: This firm has been in exisTENce for TEN years.

_____

_____

Trace: *existence*

_____

Sentences: **Existence** is the first desire of mankind.

Central plumbing was not **existent** at the time.

The exercise of free will is an **existential** principle.

FOURTH WEEK REVIEW: 10 Sentences on Saturday

1. **Conscience** makes cowards of us all.
2. **Authority** should rest with the wise and just.
3. **Benefit** yourself by checking the value.
4. The **basis** for his action was the report.
5. **Existence** is the first desire of mankind.
6. If you are **conscientious,** you will succeed.
7. I object to your **authoritarian** tone.
8. The outcome proved to be **beneficial.**
9. The **basic** idea was sound.
10. Central plumbing was not **existent** at the time.

5 Sentences on Sunday

1. It was a **conscious** act of violence.
2. We studied the **authoritative** document.
3. Who has **benefited** from the loan?
4. Their vote shows that they are **basically** opposed.
5. The exercise of free will is an **existential** principle.

Monthly Review Paragraphs

I.

The **existence** of the mail order catalog has been of **benefit** to many people for years. **Government** workers, whose **financial** position is often a **casualty** of inflation, can buy **necessary** items at fair prices because the **basis** upon which the company operates is **quantity** sales, **excellent** materials, and low profit **requirements**. To **determine** the **definite** aid this type of selling is to others as well, one may read the **recommendations** that appear in a **bulletin** by a consumer organization whose **authority** and **cooperation** are appreciated by persons of good **sense**. On one **occasion**, an **acquaintance** of mine remarked that business through the mails tested the **conscience** of the seller.

II.

After the **casualties** had been **determined, bulletins** were issued to announce the **basic** fact that the **authoritarian** ruler had been removed. The new congress was **recommending** a head of state whose mark of **excellence** would be a **conscientious** effort to eliminate **existent** differences, develop a **financially** sound budget, and create a climate in which citizens are **cooperating** because their **required** needs are being met by **beneficial** programs. Those who were **acquainted** with the former conditions were **definitely** convinced of the **necessity** for a **sensible** change if the area were to be made **governable**. Among the **quantities** of editorials in the newspapers, only an **occasional** one was critical.

III.

The **governor** had ordered all post offices **bulletined** with a picture of the **financier** who had refused to **cooperate** in the investigation, thus **requiring** some means of **acquainting** the local police with the missing witness. Even believers in **existential** principles could not find **recommendable** the actions of anyone who **casually** defied an **authoritative** committee that was **necessarily conscious** of its duty to make a **determination** of who had **benefited** from the stock fraud. It was hard to **define** the scope of the **sensitive** issue, but the **quantitative** losses of the investors were **basically** clear. Too often, rather than **occasionally,** those who **excel** in promoting dishonest schemes seek to escape by flight.

· IX ·

General Program

If you completed the *thirty-day trial* **successfully, you** proved to yourself that you can become a good speller. Of course, you still need to proceed with additional weekly and monthly sessions to wipe out the rest of your personal list of troublesome words. Moreover, you will occasionally meet new words to master. But now you know how to go about it. Here is a ten-step program that should help you on the way:

1. Get a looseleaf notebook. Divide it into three sections. Reserve the first section for any word you use frequently and misspell almost always. Arrange the words as was done in the "Thirty-Day Trial." Give each entry "The Treatment."

    Label the middle pages "Rarely Used—Like to Know." These will be words you hear now and then, but are not the bread and butter of your daily language diet. Save them for a time when you can be selective about adding to your stock.

    In the final section, list the words you have mastered. Set them up in groups of ten under the heading "Mastered List." When you have accumulated a group of ten words, compose a paragraph—a story, description, anything—using the former demons. Occasionally ask someone to dictate what you have written, so that you can test yourself. Any time you misspell a word in this section, put it back to the beginning, and start all over again with it. Any error shows that you haven't established the correct habit yet.

2. Take your time. Never handle more than **one word a day.** Remember also that a few minutes at a time spread over three periods of the day are far better than six minutes spent all at once. That's worth repeating: 3 minutes in the morning, 1½ in the afternoon, and 1½ in the evening—*six minutes a day are all you need to master any word.*

3. Practice writing words **without stopping in the middle for any reason.** Trust your hand. If you have the right habit, you will spell the word right. If not, put the word in section I of your notebook, and give it "The Treatment." That old saying applies perfectly to spelling: "He who hesitates is lost."

4. Write legibly. Don't worry about the beautiful kind of handwriting few of us can imitate. But if you want to write an *e,* let there be no doubt it is an *e.* Every letter should be clear. Mechanical accuracy will increase your confidence.

5. After you complete any piece of writing, reread it with care, even if it is a note dashed off in pencil. So-called typographical errors are errors just the same.

6. Once you master a word, use it often. This will help

you practice. And you will prove to yourself that you are no longer afraid of misspelling.

7. If you find crossword puzzles amusing, by all means work them. You probably rarely remember a new word from them, but they do offer good spelling review. Word-building games can be helpful, too.

8. When you listen to the radio, or watch television, keep a pad nearby. Write some of the words you hear, especially those you've had trouble spelling before. *Do this as you listen!* If you can write the words correctly while you are concentrating on a program, they are yours for a lifetime.

9. Watch your speech. If someone says a word differently from the way you pronounce it, look it up. Remember the case of Mr. D., the man with the automobile accessories stores? His spoken mistakes came to roost in his writing.

10. Don't quit! You may be full of fight for a few weeks. Then you may get that letdown feeling. Don't give in. You can do this job easily, quickly—if you get stubborn about it.

*   *   *

Incidentally, learning to spell properly isn't all drudgery. You can have fun with words, too. The next four chapters will present some of the interesting facts in the background of modern spelling. They will show you how to trace word histories, will give you a few amusing examples of mistakes careless spellers make, and will introduce a *new spelling game.*

Each chapter is not intended as the final word on the subject it outlines. You should, however, be able to use the material as suggestions for further investigation on your own. You will improve your spelling and enjoy many hours of pleasant reading.

Tittle Page
A Handcfull
of pleasant delites
Containing sundrie new sonets
and delectable histories, in
divers kindes of Meeter.

Newly devised to the newest tunes
that are now in use, to be sung:
everie Sonet orderly pointed
to his proper Tune.

With new additions of certain Songs,
to verie late devised Notes not
Commonly Knowen, not
used heretofore.

By Clement Robinson
and divers others

AT LONDON

Printed by Richard Lhones: dwel-
ling at the signe of the Rose
and Crowne, neare
Holburne Bridge
1584

· X ·

Spelling Long Ago

To the left is what an old song sheet published over three hundred and fifty years ago looked like. Can you find the fifteen misspellings, according to today': standards? Notice the strange use of capital letters. You may well wonder how the printer kept his job.

In fact, Mr. Lhones was simply spelling as he pleased. But there were no accepted authorities then, and each writer or printer was free to be his own dictionary. For instance, you could even beat Shakespeare in a modern spelling bee. Here is the first page of his greatest play. What fifteen words would a modern teacher mark wrong?

The Tragicall Historie of

HAMLET

Prince of Denmarke

Enter two Centinels (now called Bernardo & Francisco)

1. Stand: who is that?
2. Tis I.
1. O you come most carefully upon your watch,
2. And if you meete Marcellus and Horatio
   The partners of my watch, bid them make haste.
1. I will: See who goes there.

Hor. Friends to this ground.
Mar. And leegemen to the Dane
     O farewell honest souldier, who hath releeved you?
1. Barnardo hath my place, give you good night
Mar. Holla, Barnardo.
2. Say, is Horatio there?
Hor. A peece of him.
2. Welcome Horatio, welcome good Marcellus.
Mar. What hath this thing appear'd againe tonight.
2. I have seene nothing.
Mar. Horatio sayes tis but our fantasie,
     And wil not let beliefe take hold of him,
     Touching this dreaded sight twice seene by us, . . .

Even the great John Milton, author of *Paradise Lost,*
would be given the dunce cap in an eighth-grade English
class today. This selection from a poem on his twenty-
third birthday is full of errors in spelling, punctuation, and
capitalization—according to the way we would write.

How soone hath Time the suttle theefe of Youth
    Stolne on his wing my three & twentith yeere
    my hasting days fly on with full careere
    but my late spring no bud or blossome shew'th

Perhapps my semblance might deceave ye truth
    that I to manhood am arriv'd so neere
    & inward ripenesse doth much lesse appeare
    that some more tymely-happie spirits indu'th

Before you start saying, "What was good enough for the
masters is good enough for me," you must realize that it
was only because the writers themselves began to try for
some sort of regularity that modern spelling emerged.
They recognized the eventual confusion that would result
from spelling by ear. By the eighteenth century, great

progress toward uniformity had been made. In one of the first magazines ever published, *The Spectator,* edited by Joseph Addison and Richard Steele, we can see fewer differences from our style of writing than existed during the reign of the first Elizabeth.

Thursday, March 1, 1711

. . . I had not been long at the University before I distinguished myself by a most profound Silence. For during the Space of eight Years, excepting in the publick Exercises of the College, I scarce uttered the Quantity of an hundred Words; and indeed do not remember that I ever spoke three Sentences together in my whole Life. . . .

By the time Boswell had stopped recording the life of Dr. Johnson in the latter half of the eighteenth century, a page of a London manuscript would have shown few surprises to us.

Oddly enough, however, we Americans took longer to straighten out our letters and punctuation marks. That is partly why some experts claim that our version of English is actually older in form than the modern British.

Less than two hundred years ago, when England was beginning to standardize its spelling, our forefathers were still spelling by ear. In this selection from a charming story about a trip to New York from Boston, Sarah Kemble Knight would have fitted in nicely with English writers who lived a hundred years before her.

I was Interogated by . . . the Eldest daughter of the family, with these . . . . words, (viz.) "Law for mee-what in the world brings You here at this time a night?—I never see a woman on the Rode so Dreadfull late, in all the days of my versall life. Who are You? Where are you going? I'me scar'd out of my witts" . . . . when in comes my Guide-to him Madam turn'd Roreing out: "Lawfull heart, John, is it You?—how de do! Where in the world are you going with this woman? Who is she?"

You will agree that loose spelling is interesting, and certainly colorful. But failure to use agreed-upon spellings eventually would have led in writing to what happened in nations where dialects became too widespread and numerous. It is not unusual for some countrymen to speak the same basic language, but fail to understand one another because of the difference in dialect.

Spelling and the Family Tree

Tracing words to their original sources can be fascinating. There are many interesting stories behind modern usage. But apart from the entertainment you can have learning the history of a particular word family, you can also gain valuable aid in your spelling problems.

For example, in the days of the Romans, when a man was an officeseeker he was required to wear a white toga, or robe, to let the people know that he was anxious for their votes. *Candidus* is the Latin term for "robed in white." Hence, we have the present use of the word *candidate* for one who is trying to be elected.

Knowing this fact can help you establish a bond with the difficult part of the word, in this case the *did* syllable. Thus, while a good association is always useful, an enriched understanding of the meaning is so much the better.

Here are some additional derivations that make good reading as well as strong bonds. Get into the habit of checking the family tree of every word you look up. It might sound silly if you told someone you spent a few hours "reading" the dictionary. But in fact, it can be as much fun as a novel.

ABUNDANCE. This is also from the Latin *ab* (from) and *unda* (wave). Because water is very plentiful, anything appearing in wavelike quantities would be abundant. Note the *a* in *unda* as a bond for *ance*.

ADJECTIVE. Here it is *ad* (toward, at) and *jacere* (to throw). These words are literally thrown at others (nouns) to make them clearer or more colorful. The *dj* combination stands out this way, doesn't it?

ALPHABET. The first two letters in Greek are *alpha* and *beta*. The word therefore means nothing more than the *"a, b's."* Note the *ph* in *alpha* for your spelling aid.

BARBAROUS. The Greeks thought any language other than their own crude, rough, uncivilized. They referred to strange foreign sounds as *bar-bar*, nonsense sounds. Note how the first two syllables of the word are merely repeats, thus helping you remember the two *a's*.

BOYCOTT. Captain Boycott was an agent for an Irish landlord whose rents were very high. The collector was subjected to social isolation as a protest by the people. Somehow we seem to remember the spelling of a name more readily than some words, so that perhaps you will not forget to use the double *t* when you write *boycott*.

CHAUVINISM. Nicholas Chauvin was a member of Napoleon's army, and he was so intensely patriotic that gradually he became a joke among his associates. Spelling the name right helps you over the major hurdle in the word.

DAHLIA. The Swedish botanist, *Dahl*, had this flower named after him. Don't leave that *h* out!

DISASTROUS. We go back to Latin for *dis* (against) and *astra* (stars); anything happening contrary to the stars, or good fortune, would be *disastrous.* Note the *tr* combination in *astra.* Don't put any letter between the two when you write the word.

DUFFEL. This came from a town in England where a type of rough woollen cloth was made. Today, the duffel bag is made of canvas, but the spelling of the town is still with us.

EXHILARATE. Again we are in ancient Rome, where we meet *ex* (out of) and *hilaris* (cheerful); anything that produces a good feeling **exhilarates.** Note the *lar,* and keep the *a* there.

EXORBITANT. This really means "out of the orbit," or unusually above the average. Start with *ex,* add *orbit,* and there you are.

INNUENDO. *In* (toward) plus *nuere* (to nod) combine to give us a word that applies to a statement that doesn't make its point directly but sort of nods in the right direction. You can see where we get the two *n's.*

LISTERINE. It was easy for this product to take the name of the English scientist, Lord Lister, and make a word out of it.

LUNATIC. You can remember the *a* in this word by recalling that it comes from *luna* (the moon). An old superstition claimed that one who stared at the moon would go mad.

MACADAM. The Scottish engineer who thought of

a new road-surfacing material lent his name to the product.

MAUSOLEUM. In 353 B.C., the wife of King Mausolus ordered a magnificent monument erected in his memory. Start with the name, and the rest is easy.

MESMERIZE. F. A. Mesmer, an Austrian doctor and hypnotist, found his name attached to the technique of causing people to fall asleep or lose their wills. The name itself isn't hard at all.

NICOTINE. Jacques Nicot, the French ambassador at Lisbon, sent some plants back to one of the De-Medicis. Judging from modern advertising, he didn't do us a favor, because he's the one (at least in the word) we try to get rid of. Note the *ot*.

PANDEMONIUM. When a home run is hit and pandemonium reigns, the place is really full (*pan*) of demons (*demonium*). Put the demon in the middle, and you chase his spelling friends away.

QUARANTINE. Formerly, when a person had a communicable disease, he was required to stay indoors for forty (*quaranta*) days. Today, the period is shorter, but the *ara* combination has not changed.

SACRILEGE. Some shady customers used to like to collect (*legere*) sacred (*sacri*) objects. The trouble was that they didn't bother to ask anyone's permission, and now *sacrilege*, with the *e* from *leg*, implies an act or statement against religious beliefs.

VULCANIZE. The Roman god *Vulcan* would forge

and hammer weapons for his fellow inhabitants of the clouds. Now he has been reduced to a tire patch.

WORSTED. This is just the name of an English town, and the *r* is a typical silent British letter.

ZINNIA. The German botanist, J. G. Zinn, has been immortalized by this lovely flower. Note the double *n*.

Of course, these twenty-five examples are but a handful of the thousands of word histories waiting for you to uncover their mysteries. And more often than not, the illogical modern spelling is the result of the odd names and language combinations that were taken bodily into our collection. This is one more time that you can look to the ancestors for the faults in the descendants.

• XII •

Spelling Boners

Ordinarily, when you've been guilty of a misspelling, there is nothing to laugh about. You are seriously concerned about the word, and you should add it to the list that is the basis of your personal study program. However, now and then you may discover that the error has resulted in a rather amusing sentence, especially when the wrong form suggests another word that changes the meaning entirely.

You ought to enjoy these taken from examination papers, newspaper columns, letters, reports, and similar materials. After you've had a chuckle or two, consider how easily all the mistakes, frequently the result of only carelessness, could have been eliminated simply by a more careful rereading before release to the reader.

Watch out for these "boners." Check what you write. If you find something to laugh about in your work, get rid of it before anyone else sees it. Here are some samples. In the *second sentence* for each pair, the word is used correctly.

*   *   *

Paul was visibly **infected** by her words.
She wasn't the least **affected** by his, however.

*   *   *

The cab driver was **carousing** all over town, looking for a fare.

And a police car was **cruising** around looking for him.

* * *

He was a **stench** upholder of fair play.

So **staunch** a principle should not be suppressed.

* * *

The Arabs had nothing but the **dessert** to live on, so they didn't have enough to eat.

What else can one grow on a **desert?**

* * *

Louis XVI was **gelatined** by the Jacobins.

After he was **guillotined,** of course!

* * *

His signature was so **eligible** that the bank refused to cash his check.

Besides, his handwriting was **illegible!**

* * *

She was **tide** up all morning.

And she came out cleaner than any soap, with one hand **tied** behind her back.

* * *

Many of our colonies were founded by people who had been **executed.**

Afterward, they were **exiled.**

*   *   *

Salt Lake City is a place where the **Morons** settled.
The **Mormons** weren't too happy about them.

*   *   *

Mr. Kent's favorite meal was **stake** smothered in **unions.**
On the other hand, the president of the local preferred **steak** with **onions.**

*   *   *

The batter hit a **fowl** that went clear out of the park.
I'll bet he suspected **foul** play.

*   *   *

Beginning of a letter: "Dear **Anut** Sally."
Really, frankness can go just so far, even with an **aunt!**

*   *   *

It was just to make sure that no one would **enroach** on his territory.
Nor did he want to **encroach** on theirs.

*   *   *

Spellagrams

You have probably tried your hand at crossword puzzles, anagrams, cryptograms, and other word games. However, most of these are not very helpful for sharpening spelling habits. Either there is too much to do or sufficient stress is not laid on letter combinations directly.

The **SPELLAGRAM** has been designed to be of value *especially* to those who have spelling problems. Once you have gotten the general idea, you'll find it both instructive and fun. You can make the **SPELLAGRAM** a fascinating parlor game. We'll tell you how later. And, by the way, there are three forms!

Spellagram—Form A

10
N E C I N E C O S C

_ _ _ _ _ _ _ _ _ _
(one's inner self)

7
D R O B I F S

_ _ _ _ _ _ _
(prohibits)

7
C L A S P I E

_ _ _ _ _ _ _
(particular)

10
G R E E L I V I S P

_ _ _ _ _ _ _ _ _ _
(favors, advantages)

Rules

1. The four blanks represent words that form a telegram message. Each space in the blank is for one letter.

2. Above the blank is the word that belongs in the spaces, but it is in scrambled form.

3. Below the blank is the definition of the word. This is to give you a hint.

4. Your job is simply to use the meanings to help you unscramble the words, so that the message reads correctly. In this case, you would finally arrive at **CONSCIENCE FORBIDS SPECIAL PRIVILEGES.**

5. Note that *every letter in the scrambled word must be used.* Cross each one out as you place it in its proper space.

6. If you have used all the letters, but in the wrong order, you are charged with a misspelling.

7. The scoring is easy. Count the letters in the word missed, and subtract the sum from the total number of letters in the message. For example, this one has 34 letters in all. If you had missed **PRIVILEGES,** you would take 10 from 34, leaving you with the final score of 24.

Spellagram—Form B

This is the second form of the game.

8   8

_ _ _ _ _ _ _ _   _ _ _ _ _ _ _ _
(set apart)   (accommodations)

9   11

_ _ _ _ _ _ _ _ _   _ _ _ _ _ _ _ _ _ _ _
(usable, at hand)   (at once, now)

A A A A A A A	I I I	Q	U
B	L L L	R R R	V
D	M M	S S	Y
E E E E E	P	T T T	

Rules

1. The number above the blank indicates how many letters there are in the word.

2. As in Form A, the definitions below the blanks are hints about the words needed to complete the message.

3. Below the puzzle are listed the letters to be used in filling in the spaces.

4. When you have decided on a word, cross out the letters required to write it, and put the word in the blank.

5. Do this until you have completed the message.

6. Naturally, if you have misspelled any words, you will find a shortage of some letters or too many of others. Thus, you will be forced to check your work. Remember: *all letters must have been crossed out when you have finished.*

7. Here, too, you score by deducting the number of letters of each wrong word from the grand total. For example, this message is: **SEPARATE QUARTERS AVAILABLE IMMEDIATELY,** 36 letters in all. If you misspelled **SEPARATE,** your score is 36 less 8, or 28.

You can form teams among your friends. Each side makes up the **SPELLAGRAMS** for the other, or a neutral party does the work for both sides. Here's how you keep score:

1. In any series or round, the **SPELLAGRAM** for both sides must have the same number of letters.

2. Time the period it takes each team to work out the **SPELLAGRAM.**

3. Make the usual deductions for errors in spelling as outlined above.

4. Add the difference in time it takes one group to finish as compared to the other.

5. Suppose Team A finishes the puzzle accurately in 3 minutes, and Team B in 5 minutes. In a 36-letter game, the final score would be 38-36 in favor of A. Of course, misspellings would further affect the score.

Spellagram—Form C

1. The basic game takes two players. Each player has a pad of paper and a pencil. Also, one of the players should have a watch. The player to go first is chosen by the flip of a coin or the drawing of a card.

2. Player A, the first player, selects a word. He then records the word on one slip of paper (out of sight of his opponent), and on another slip of paper, he writes the word in scrambled form.

3. At the word "Go!" player A gives the scrambled word to player B.

4. Player B has two minutes to work out the word. If he manages to get the original word, he gets the full number of points corresponding to the number of letters. If he gets another word but still uses up all the letters of the scrambled word, he gets credit for the number of letters minus 1. If he cannot discover a word that uses all the letters, he tries to make any word or words he can, with as many letters as he can. He then gets credit for the number of letters used. But any misspellings mean a zero score for the round.

5. Player B now composes his word and gives it in scrambled form to A. However, he must use *the same number of letters* player A used.

6. The player who has the highest score at the end of each round has the advantage of leading off the next round. If the players are tied, the advantage remains with the same player until his opponent has a higher score.

7. Score is kept on the basis of points, and the player who first arrives at 100 or more points wins the game.

8. The game can also be played by four people, two

against two, with partners working on the scrambled words.

Here is the start of a sample game:

1. Player A wins the toss.

2. He now selects **SMATTER** (7 letters), for example, as his word. He writes **SMATTER** on one piece of paper, and on another he writes **RASETMT** (a scrambled form of **SMATTER**).

3. At the word "Go!" A gives B the slip of paper with the scrambled word form, and B now has two minutes to unscramble the word.

4. If, within two minutes, B gets **SMATTER,** he is credited with 7 full points (one for each letter in the original word). If he chooses **MATTERS**, he gets 6 points. (He has used all the letters but has not guessed the right word!) If he gets **MASTER**, he gets 6 points. (There is still one T left over.) If he can think of only **MATE** or **MAST**, he gets only 4 points. If he misspells, he gets 0 points.

5. It is now B's turn to give a word to A. B chooses **COLLEGE** (another 7-letter word) and passes on **GLELEOC** to A, who has two minutes to see what he can do with that patchwork of letters. And so the game progresses. Remember: the next words can be ten letters or eight letters or any number just so that the opponents use words of the same length in each round.

Here are some additional **SPELLAGRAMS** for Forms A and B:

Additional Spellagrams—Form A

1.

10
NOVEMTNERG

_____
(rule)

14
CANTREMINOMODE

_____
(statement favoring)

11
TUBELDOYNDU

_____
(unquestionably)

10
PACLABEECT

_____
(welcome)

2.

14
DENENTRUSPENIT

_____
(person in charge)

9
PLIGELENX

_____
(ejecting)

11
COMESHISUVI

_____
(full of tricks)

9
TRIMYOORD

_____
(rooms in college)

9
SPUTACONC

_____
(dwellers)

3.

10
ETOOBULAIM

_____

(four-wheeled car)

7
TIXBIHE

_____

(show)

9
NIGENBING

_____

(starting)

9
DEWSNEADY

_____

(fourth day)

10
GOTINCINUN

_____

(lasting)

8
GRASTHIT

_____

(not bent)

7
HOGHURT

_____

(end to end)

8
YARRBUEF

_____

(very cold one)

Spellagrams—Form B

1.

                   9   11

———————————   ———————————

(chosen group)   (assuredly)

                   7   8

———————   ———————

(looks for)   (full)

                 10

———————————

(being present)

A A A A	F	N N N N	T T T T T T
C C C C C	I I I	O O	X
D D	L	P P	Y Y
E E E E E E	M M	S	

8   5

2.

_ _ _ _ _ _ _ _   _ _ _ _ _
(trade)   (time measure)

                        10   7

_ _ _ _ _ _ _ _ _ _   _ _ _ _ _ _ _
(kept running)   (notwithstanding)

                        6   11

_ _ _ _ _ _   _ _ _ _ _ _ _ _ _ _ _ _
(every 365 days)   (holiday observance)

AAAAA	EEEEE	M	RR
BB	H	NNNNN	SSSSS
C	IIIII	OO	TTT
DD	LL	P	UUU

3.

7   14

_ _ _ _ _ _ _   _ _ _ _ _ _ _ _ _ _ _ _ _ _

(not native)   (delegate)

9   8

_ _ _ _ _ _ _ _ _   _ _ _ _ _ _ _ _

(warmly)   (presenting)

9   9

_ _ _ _ _ _ _ _ _   _ _ _ _ _ _ _ _ _

(very good)   (of money)

11

_ _ _ _ _ _ _ _ _ _ _

(working together)

AAAAA	FFFF	NNNNNNNS
CCCC	GG	OOOOOO TTTT
D	IIIIIIPP	V
EEEEEEEEEE	LLLLLRRRRRR	X
		Y

ANSWERS

Form A—1. Government recommendation undoubtedly acceptable.

2. Superintendent expelling mischievous dormitory occupants.

3. Automobile exhibit beginning Wednesday continuing straight through February.

Form B—1. Committee confidently expects capacity attendance.

2. Business hours maintained despite annual celebration.

3. Foreign representative cordially offering excellent financial cooperation.

· XIV ·

Variant Spellings

When you are in doubt about a word, you ordinarily consult a dictionary to check the spelling, usually printed in **boldface** type at the beginning of the entry. While this procedure settles the problem for the vast majority of words, it does not always work so simply. Occasionally, your dictionary will list a particular spelling first and then include alternate or *variant spellings* as well. There wouldn't be much to be concerned about if we could say flatly that the first listing is always the "preferred" spelling and that any others are sometimes used but are not really acceptable. But it would be incorrect to make such a statement—for a very good reason. Dictionaries do not always agree!

Let's use a relatively simple word as our example. In a study made among five excellent dictionaries, *mama* was listed first in three of them and *mamma* as a variant in two, but *mamma* was listed first in two of them and *mama* thus became the variant. It seems clear, then, that for certain words the preferred spelling will depend upon the particular dictionary you are using as your reference. Doesn't this situation add to your problems in your efforts to become a good speller? It would seem so, but I can suggest an approach that will help you avoid confusion.

First, however, we should analyze why the listing of

135

spellings, where more than one exists, is not always uniform. A dictionary simply records what the editors of an edition consider to be common usage among respected writers *at the time the dictionary is published*. Because language changes as time goes on, each new edition of a dictionary reflects the changes. Not only are new words added and some old words reclassified, but revisions are made in pronunciations and spellings.

Unfortunately, there is no single dictionary, among the dozens published in this country, that can be called "standard" or "official." Thus, the editors compiling the lists and definitions for the various publishers have complete freedom in deciding what is common usage. Obviously, disagreement among the word experts is inevitable. That's why preferred spellings in one dictionary become variants in another. The judgment of editors determines listings, therefore, not the findings of some central authoritative source.

A very good treatment of the problem can be found in *Variant Spellings in Modern American Dictionaries* (revised edition), by Donald W. Emery, a publication of the National Council of Teachers of English. For his research, Emery used desk copies of the following dictionaries:

1. *The American Heritage Dictionary of the English Language,* Heritage Publishing Co., Inc.
2. *Webster's New Collegiate Dictionary,* Eighth Edition, G. & C. Merriam Co.
3. *Webster's New World Dictionary of the American Language,* Second College Edition, World Publishing Co.
4. *The Random House College Dictionary,* Random House, Inc.
5. *Standard College Dictionary,* Text Edtion, Funk and Wagnalls.

A few examples from the Emery booklet should give you some idea of how dictionaries disagree in their listings of words that have more than one spelling. The word *cozy*, as spelled, is listed first in all five dictionaries. However, *cosy* is also a variant in all of them, and two of them in each example list further variants: *cosey, cozey, cosie, cozie!* Indeed, in the following admittedly artificial sentence, the quantity of variants for each word in **boldface** is listed in parentheses:

In a **cozy** (5) house **cater-cornered** (5) from the palace, a **finicky** (7) **caliph** (5), who maintained that a **jinni** or **genie** (8) had revealed to him the secrets of the **cabala** (5), spent much time smoking **panatelas** (4)—sometimes **kef** (4)—and training his pet **parakeet** (5).

Only the spellings used for *cozy, finicky, caliph, cabala,* and *parakeet* are listed first in all five dictionaries. Emery concludes that one could write the sentence in 11,197,440 ways, with no two versions exactly alike!

Not only do the variants pop up for isolated words but they also occur in fair abundance when covered by even the few supposedly reliable rules previously discussed. You have learned, for instance, that a word ending in a vowel—*use*—generally loses its final vowel when another syllable beginning with a vowel is added, thus *usable*. The latter spelling does appear first in all the dictionaries cited. But *useable* is a variant in all, too! Similar "rule-breaking" can be found with *plurals* (*banjos-banjoes*), *compounds* (*attorneys-general, attorney-generals*) *full* endings (*armfuls-armsful*), *able, ible* endings (*collectible-collectable*), *er, or* endings (*adviser-advisor*), *y* endings (*flier-flyer*), the *FSA* group (*bused-bussed, diagramed-diagrammed*), and so-called British or other national influences (*glamorous-glamourous*).

At this point, you must be wondering whether any spelling is ever right or wrong. Rest assured that for most words there is only one acceptable spelling. Variants are listed for fewer than ½ of 1 percent of all the words in our language. If this is so, what should you do about the variants?

Certainly, the worst thing you can do is to permit the variants to confuse you. *Remember that every spelling previously given for random words or those covered by the useful rules is absolutely acceptable, as is the spelling of every word in the lists printed in the Appendix.* The policy here has been to print only those spellings that appear first in the majority of good dictionaries. You still, therefore, need to master only one form of the spelling of a word. If you don't already own one, get a desk copy of a good dictionary and use it—and it alone—as your authority. That's it. Forget about the variants. Only after you have become a truly master speller should you seek to satisfy your curiosity about how many different ways a word can be spelled.

On the other hand, if the suggestion is to ignore the variants, why was this chapter included at all? For one thing, your study of spelling would be incomplete unless you were aware of the existence of variants. Such awareness should convince you that no one can be dogmatic or rigid about the spelling of certain words. Before you decide that a spelling you have seen is "wrong," check it with a dictionary. If you find the strange spelling listed as a variant, it must be regarded as acceptable. However, this doesn't mean that you should change your own manner of spelling the word. If the form you have been using is listed first in your dictionary, stay with it.

One exception to the recommended practice must be noted. Should you some day decide to enter the National

Spelling Bee, you would be bound by the rule governing the contest:

> *Webster's Third New International Dictionary,* of its most recent copyright date, G. & C. Merriam Co., shall serve as the final authority for the spellings of words in the national finals. If a word has two or more accepted spellings, only the spellings set in boldface type and separated by the word *OR,* and in some cases the word *ALSO,* at the beginning of the descriptive matter will be accepted as correct. Words having the labels *ARCHAIC* and *OBSOLETE* (abbreviated OBS.) and regional labels (like *NORTH, SOUTH, BRITISH, IRISH*) will not be accepted as correct.

About Word Lists

The words that appear in the *Appendix* **that follows** have been carefully selected after considerable research into various studies that have evaluated words in terms of the following factors:

1. the grade level at which a word is normally introduced;

2. the frequency with which the word appears in reading, listening, speaking, and writing activities;

3. the relative "difficulty" of a word as evidenced by how often it is misspelled by significant numbers of writers on all levels.

However, in working with the various lists, you should bear these points in mind:

1. The only source that contains every word you are likely to meet is an unabridged dictionary with over 600,000 entries. Obviously, then, in a collection of 2500 words, the range is extremely limited and represents samples rather than absolute choices.

2. No two research studies have ever been found to agree precisely. The reasons are quite simple. As has been

stated in the preceding text, word difficulty is a personal matter. What is hard for one person to spell may offer no problem at all for another. Moreover, words that are used frequently in one region may be used less often elsewhere. Indeed, one study showed that, in two schools less than a mile apart, there was wide variation in word frequency and difficulty!

3. The lists that follow, therefore, are neither better nor worse than lists you might find in other spelling books. The important thing to remember is that you have learned how to master the spelling of any word, regardless of whether or not it appears on a particular list. Use the material in the *Appendix* for self-diagnosis, practice, and the development of the confidence you need to become a master speller. In the long run, the most reliable list you can use is the one you develop on your own as you accumulate words that must be given "The Treatment" (see p. 73) by you.

*　　　　*　　　　*

In the current revision of this book, certain changes were made in the lists to include words that have become important in recent years, typical examples being *racism, feminist, fission, videotape, telemetry, ballistics,* and *laser.* Also, some words have been dropped so that others of equal frequency of use or challenge might be included. Let me point out again that even the revised lists represent only samples and are not intended to suggest that the final entries have anything all-inclusive about them.

Appendix

This section contains 2500 selected words. You will note that they have been divided into three groups—**basic** (including "100 Spelling Demons"), **average**, and **advanced**. This has been done to enable you to find out for yourself just where you fit in terms of general ability.

If you can spell all in the **basic** list, you are doing about as well as a person with an elementary school background. A score of 100 percent in the **average** group indicates that you can hold your own with most people, regardless of their educational training. After you have achieved complete accuracy with the **advanced** words, you will be able to call yourself a superior speller.

Go through each list systematically. Have someone dictate the diagnostic sentences to you, or play the appropriate tape or cassette if you have managed to prepare one. As soon as you have accumulated twenty words that require further study, take one a day for a month as described in the "Thirty-Day Trial." Test the results of your planned attack, and if you make no mistakes, go on to the next group of sentences. In general, then, it is TEST, STUDY, TEST.

Incidentally, the sentences that accompany the lists contain words that have been deliberately inserted to increase the diagnostic range. Therefore, if you *misspell any word in a sentence,* regardless of whether or not it appears in the alphabetized list, add it to your personal list of words that need further attention.

Diagnostic Sentences

1–25

1. We **can't choose** the **blue color again.**
2. The **country doctor** is **always busy among** his people.
3. I **believe** this **business** is **dear** to him because he **built** it from the **beginning.**
4. If the **cough does** make your chest **ache, buy** something to **break** it up.
5. There **could** not have **been any answer** to why he was **coming.**

26–50

1. Learn **grammar early enough** and you will find it **easy** to **know** what is correct.
2. I **heard** a **hoarse** voice and **knew** that my **friend** was **here.**
3. **Instead** of trying to **guess, just** try to **hear every** word.
4. The digging **done,** he **laid** the bulbs in **loose** soil and watered them for **half** an **hour.**
5. **Don't lose** sight of the fact that they are **having forty** people to dinner in **February.**

Basic List

100 Spelling Demons

1–25	26–50
ache	done
again	don't
always	early
among	easy
answer	enough
any	every
been	February
beginning	forty
believe	friend
blue	grammar
break	guess
built	half
business	having
busy	hear
buy	heard
can't	here
choose	hoarse
color	hour
coming	instead
cough	just
could	knew
country	know
dear	laid
doctor	loose
does	lose

Diagnostic Sentences

51–75

1. It **seems** that children can **tear their** new **shoes** in a **minute.**
2. **There** is a **separate piece** of **sugar ready** for your tea.
3. **Some said** the **raise** was **sure** to come at **once.**
4. He **often says** he **meant** to **read** it **many** times.
5. **Making** a **straight** line was **much** harder **since none** of them had a ruler.

76–100

1. **Each week,** on **Tuesday** and **Wednesday,** the **women used** to sell old clothes.
2. **Though very tired,** I'm **writing tonight.**
3. **They wrote** to ask **whether** or not the **two** boys **would** come.
4. I am **truly too** busy to **write** about the dress **which** I will **wear.**
5. **There won't** be any **trouble** if it is sent **through** the store **where** the **whole** record is kept.

Basic List Continued

100 Spelling Demons

51–75	76–100
making	they
many	though
meant	through
minute	tired
much	tonight
none	too
often	trouble
once	truly
piece	Tuesday
raise	two
read	used
ready	very
said	wear
says	Wednesday
seems	week
separate	where
shoes	whether
since	which
some	whole
straight	women
sugar	won't
sure	would
tear	write
their	writing
there	wrote

Diagnostic Sentences

101–125

1. Struck by the **automobile,** the **angry animal** ran **across** the **avenue.**
2. The **advertisement** gave the **amount** of salary and the **address** where those **already** eighteen could **apply.**
3. Since the **accident,** the poor boy has been **absent** and pays **almost** no **attention** to the **alphabet.**
4. **Although** he may not be **around** before late **August** or early **autumn,** we can **appoint** him anyway.
5. At the **army** post last **April,** my **aunt** slipped on a **banana** peel and fell **against** a wall.

126–150

1. The **butcher** sold a **certain** kind of **chicken** at a **cheap** price to **build** up his trade.
2. My brother was **calm** when he took the **chalk** at the **blackboard** and drew a man with a **beautiful beard.**
3. Be **careful** to put the **candle** near the **chair** away from the **bottom** of the **Christmas** tree.
4. The **chief** scout put the **cheese** and a **bottle** of wine on a **board between** the weary travelers.
5. **Change** the **button because** it will rub your **cheek** if you are **careless.**

Basic List Continued

101–125	126–150
absent	beard
accident	beautiful
across	because
address	between
advertisement	blackboard
against	board
almost	bottle
alphabet	bottom
already	build
although	butcher
amount	button
angry	calm
animal	candle
apply	careful
appoint	careless
April	certain
army	chair
around	chalk
attention	change
August	cheap
aunt	cheek
automobile	cheese
autumn	chicken
avenue	chief
banana	Christmas

Diagnostic Sentences

151–175

1. The **death** of the **conductor** in **December** caused the **company** to **close** the tour.
2. A good **citizen** knows the **danger** that **cities** face when they fail to **collect court** fines.
3. The tired **dentist** poured **cream** into his **coffee,** ate a **cracker,** lit a **cigarette,** and took out his **comb.**
4. We must **decide** on a **correct collar** for the **cotton** dress or the **customer** will not buy it.
5. Her **daughter** went to **church** to help her **cousin** count the **copies** of the new prayer books.

176–200

1. We **expect** to pay a **dollar** and **eighty** cents for **dinner** this **evening.**
2. There are **eight different** parts to each **exercise except** the **eleventh.**
3. **Eighteen** people came to **examine** the **empty** houses and a **dozen** left a **deposit.**
4. Two men **died** some **distance** from the **entrance** to the **factory** when a mound of **earth** fell on them.
5. **Either** his **education** in **English** during the **eighth** year had been poor or he had forgotten **everything.**

Basic List Continued

151–175	**176–200**
church	deposit
cigarette	died
cities	different
citizen	dinner
close	distance
coffee	dollar
collar	dozen
collect	earth
comb	education
company	eight
conductor	eighteen
copies	eighth
correct	eighty
cotton	either
court	eleventh
cousin	empty
cracker	English
cream	entrance
customer	evening
danger	everything
daughter	examine
death	except
December	exercise
decide	expect
dentist	factory

Diagnostic Sentences

201–225

1. I am looking **forward** to using the **fourth Friday** as a happy **holiday** and will buy **flour** to bake a cake.
2. Her **husband** planted the **flower** in the **garden** to avoid a **family fight.**
3. The **hospital** announced that the **grocery** clerk had been hit on the **forehead** with a **heavy** object like a **hammer.**
4. If they are **hungry, fifteen grown** boys can eat a **gallon** of ice cream in **fourteen** seconds.
5. The initials on the **handkerchief** were a **great** help in proving the **forger** had used a **foreign** name to pass a **hundred** bad checks.

226–250

1. **June** began to **learn** to **laugh** a **little** in **kindergarten.**
2. They will **marry** in **January** or **March,** and there is much **interest** in the **match.**
3. The **length** of the **language lesson** does not **matter,** so long as you **listen.**
4. It is **known** that a **loaf** of bread from the home **kitchen** will supply a good **measure** of **iron.**
5. Writing a **letter** in the **light** of a lazy **July** day will **knock** any idea of **labor** out of your mind.

Basic List Continued

201–225	**226–250**
family	interest
fifteen	iron
fight	January
flour	July
flower	June
forehead	kindergarten
foreign	kitchen
forger	knock
forward	known
fourteen	labor
fourth	language
Friday	laugh
gallon	learn
garden	length
great	lesson
grocery	letter
grown	light
hammer	listen
handkerchief	little
heavy	loaf
holiday	March
hospital	marry
hundred	match
hungry	matter
husband	measure

Diagnostic Sentences

251–275

1. **Neither** my **niece** nor her **mother** thought the new **mustache** suited my **nephew**.
2. **Monday morning** the **newspaper** announced that **nineteen** men had scaled the **mountain**.
3. All **month** he kept the **medicine near** his bed because he would need it in the **middle** of the **night**.
4. Even if he didn't invest another **nickel**, his **money** would soon **multiply** into **ninety million** dollars.
5. It **might** be a bad **mistake** to put a **needle** or a **nail** into your **mouth**.

276–300

1. A **perfect picture** of an **orange, peach,** and **pear** won the prize.
2. From **October** to **November,** the company **ought** to **offer** reduced rates for the **ocean** trip.
3. **People** of that **period** could buy a **pencil** and paper for a **penny**.
4. **Nothing** was heard until two **o'clock** of the **ninth** day, when the **noise** of a **parade** told us **peace** had come.
5. Wearing his **overalls** under his **overcoat,** he brought an **ounce** or two of milk in a **pail** to ease the **pain** of the sick calf.

Basic List Continued

251–275	276–300
medicine	ninth
middle	noise
might	nothing
million	November
mistake	ocean
Monday	o'clock
money	October
month	offer
morning	orange
mother	ought
mountain	ounce
mouth	overalls
multiply	overcoat
mustache	pail
nail	pain
near	parade
needle	peace
neither	peach
nephew	pear
newspaper	pencil
nickel	penny
niece	people
night	perfect
nineteen	period
ninety	picture

Diagnostic Sentences

301–325

1. The prime **reason** for his **quest** was to **receive** a **promise** from the king to **pretend** that he was ill.
2. Do everything in your **power** to keep him **quiet,** and **please remember** to put a **pillow** under his head.
3. In a talk lasting a **quarter** of an hour, the **president** found time to **refer** to the low pay of the **postman** and **policeman.**
4. It is **possible** the **prescription** slipped from my **pocket** when I took a **quick** trip to the **post office.**
5. In the **restaurant,** the **pretty** girl had some meat with a **plain** boiled **potato,** and then drank half a **quart** of milk.

326–350

1. The **sight** of **silver** paper and colored **ribbon** made **sister** think of **Santa Claus.**
2. They **sail** on the **sixth** of September and **should** arrive in **seventeen** days.
3. Although he called over his **shoulder** for a **sandwich** several times, there was no **sign** of **service.**
4. The seal-hunting **season** started the **seventh,** and by the **sixteenth,** some **soap** and water were very welcome.
5. A desire to **sleep** cut his eyes like **scissors,** but he continued to work and **smoke** because the last **sentence** had to be written by **Saturday.**

Basic List Continued

301–325	326–350
pillow	ribbon
plain	sail
please	sandwich
pocket	Santa Claus
policeman	Saturday
possible	scissors
postman	seal
post office	season
potato	sentence
power	September
prescription	service
president	seventeen
pretend	seventh
pretty	several
promise	should
quart	shoulder
quarter	sight
quest	sign
quick	silver
quiet	sister
reason	sixteenth
receive	sixth
refer	sleep
remember	smoke
restaurant	soap

Diagnostic Sentences

351–375

1. The **Sunday** school **teacher** told every **student** that those who **suffer** are **studying** the true meaning of the **soul**.
2. **Sometimes** a **tailor** will return a **summer suit** still soiled.
3. The **soldier** sat down to a **supper** that started with **soup** and ended with **strong, sweet** wine.
4. Every **tenant** was warned by **telephone** or **telegram** that he must **sweep** his side of the **street**.
5. When you **subtract** the price of the tax **stamp**, those **stockings** from the **south** cost **something** more than ours.

376–400

1. This is **twice** that my **uncle** has left a **theater ticket** in his other **trousers**.
2. They start to **travel** on the **tenth** or **twelfth** and return by the **twentieth**, a week before **Thanksgiving**.
3. **Together** we'll pick **twelve** men **tomorrow**, and **thirteen** more next **Thursday**.
4. **Today** the rain drove **thirty thousand** people **toward** the exit gates, with not one **umbrella** among them.
5. Billy **tore** his pants, but one **touch** of a **thread** to his mother's **tongue** and they were ready for a new **trial**.

Basic List Continued

351–375	376–400
soldier	tenth
something	Thanksgiving
sometimes	theater
soul	thirteen
soup	thirty
south	thousand
stamp	thread
stockings	Thursday
street	ticket
strong	today
student	together
studying	tomorrow
subtract	tongue
suffer	tore
suit	touch
summer	toward
Sunday	travel
supper	trial
sweep	trousers
sweet	twelfth
tailor	twelve
teacher	twentieth
telegram	twice
telephone	umbrella
tenant	uncle

Diagnostic Sentences

401–425

1. The **visitor** can't **understand** how the **United States** is governed **until** he has seen **Washington.**
2. Without **warning,** a **wasp** stung the **wagon** driver who had gone for a **walk** to get some water.
3. By a **voice vote,** the group of men showed they **weren't** going to **watch** and **wait** for the **wage** conference.
4. The **warm weather** was not **usual,** and the **vegetable** crop in the **village** would grow that much sooner.
5. **While** he will let you **weigh** him, he will not **welcome** any effort to **wake** him up to the need of a trim **waist.**

426–450

1. **Yesterday** that **young woman** became the **wife** of the owner of the **zinc** mine.
2. **Your** answer was **worth zero** because you described the **wrong zone.**
3. The **zoo** was proud of the **white** fox, **whose** arrival last year had created great **wonder.**
4. On his **winter** vacation, he **woke** early every day to don his **yellow** skis and **zigzag** along the trails with the **zeal** of one who need no longer **yearn** for snowy hills.
5. **Without** a care in the **world,** he ate his dinner with great **zest,** and then looked out of his **window** as the plane began to **zoom** along at an ever faster rate.

Basic List Continued

401–425	426–450
understand	white
United States	whose
until	wife
usual	window
vegetable	winter
village	without
visitor	woke
voice	woman
vote	wonder
wage	world
wagon	worth
waist	wrong
wait	yearn
wake	yellow
walk	yesterday
warm	young
warning	your
Washington	zeal
wasp	zero
watch	zest
weather	zigzag
weigh	zinc
welcome	zone
weren't	zoo
while	zoom

Diagnostic Sentences

1–25

1. **According** to experts, an **actor** or **actress** must be born with **ability** and cannot **acquire** it.
2. **Afterward** I shall **accompany** you to the **affair** because it will be an **advantage** to **accept** this new **adventure.**
3. To go **abroad** sounded like good **advice,** but her **absence** would be an **admission** of the **actual** reason for leaving.
4. We **absolutely** cannot **acknowledge** your pass because the **addition** of secret work forces us to **abolish** former rules of **admittance.**
5. Those who adopt this **country** should develop an **accent** that people **admire,** and they can **accomplish** this by attending schools that **advertise** courses in speech.

26–50

1. So **anxious** was he to work in the **airplane** factory that any apartment near it would **appear** to be **agreeable.**
2. Blind **ambition** refuses **allegiance** even to the **altar,** and will answer any **appeal** that feeds its **appetite** for power.
3. The **amendment** to the law forced each **agency** not to **approve** or **appoint** an **applicant** who was an **alien.**
4. Your **approach** to the **argument** would be of **amusement** to **anybody** but does not **alter** the facts.
5. Tim sprained his **ankle** in the **agriculture** course and asked whether **anyone** would **arrange** to take his **arithmetic** homework to his next class.

Average List

1–25	26–50
ability	agency
abolish	agreeable
abroad	agriculture
absence	airplane
absolutely	alien
accent	allegiance
accept	altar
accompany	alter
accomplish	ambition
according	amendment
acknowledge	amusement
acquire	ankle
actor	anxious
actress	anybody
actual	anyone
addition	appeal
admire	appear
admission	appetite
admittance	applicant
advantage	appoint
adventure	approach
advertise	approve
advice	argument
affair	arithmetic
afterward	arrange

Diagnostic Sentences

51–75

1. The **arrival** of the **attorney** for the **association** caused a **battle** in the **assembly.**
2. I can **assure** you that no **attempt** will be made to **assist** you with the **baggage** until every **article** is checked.
3. With an **awful** scar on one cheek and a **bandage beneath** his eye, the **beggar** looked like a wounded **beast.**
4. The price for the **barrel** is **beyond** what it was **awhile** ago and has **become** no **bargain.**
5. Many a **backward** glance was cast at the **beefsteak** party on the **beach** as the **balance** of the group left to cast its **ballot.**

76–100

1. The boarder would beat his **breast** and **boast** that every day he read the **Bible** he kept in the hall closet.
2. You may **borrow** the **bicycle,** but don't try a **burst** of speed because the worn **brake** may earn you a **bruise.**
3. According to the **calendar,** the **cafeteria** today will serve corned beef, **cabbage,** and a **biscuit** as light as a cherry **blossom.**
4. With a **breath** of pride, Fenton recalled rising from **bootblack** to **blacksmith** to **candidate** for **bureau** chief.
5. He decided to use a **bulldozer** to **bury** the **bundle** of papers and the **cablegram** under the **bridge** and not **breathe** a word about them to the **bookkeeper.**

Average List Continued

51–75	76–100
arrival	Bible
article	bicycle
assembly	biscuit
assist	blacksmith
association	blossom
assure	boast
attempt	bookkeeper
attorney	bootblack
awful	borrow
awhile	brake
backward	breast
baggage	breath
balance	breathe
ballot	bridge
bandage	bruise
bargain	bulldozer
barrel	bundle
battle	bureau
beach	burst
beast	bury
become	cabbage
beefsteak	cablegram
beggar	cafeteria
beneath	calendar
beyond	candidate

Diagnostic Sentences

101–125

1. The **children** were ready to **celebrate** when told there was a **choice** between **cereal** and **chocolate**.
2. A **century** later, the letters of the **captain** were found in a small **carriage** left in the **cellar** of the **castle**.
3. He asked the **cashier** for **carfare** to the **capital,** where he would get the **certificate** to be a **chauffeur**.
4. A **carpenter** was sent to the upper chamber to repair a damp **circle** in the **ceiling** near the **chimney**.
5. Because it was not in his **cheerful character** to **cheat** or turn to **charity** for help, he decided to sell his **cattle** instead and be more **cautious** about money in the future.

126–150

1. To **conquer** the **climate** on the **coast, clothe** yourself in **comfortable** fashion.
2. Our **Constitution** states that only **Congress** can **consider** matters that **concern commerce**.
3. Good **citizenship** must **consist** of the desire to **complain** about any **condition** against the **common** good.
4. After the **concert,** she took her **companion** to a little shop where they could sip a cup of **cocoa** in **complete comfort**.
5. The **complaint** about the new plan of the college to **connect** the various schools is that it will **commence** before anyone can **confirm** its adoption.

Average List Continued

101–125	126–150
capital	citizenship
captain	climate
carfare	clothe
carpenter	coast
carriage	cocoa
cashier	college
castle	comfort
cattle	comfortable
cautious	commence
ceiling	commerce
celebrate	common
cellar	companion
century	complain
cereal	complaint
certificate	complete
character	concern
charity	concert
chauffeur	condition
cheat	confirm
cheerful	Congress
children	connect
chimney	conquer
chocolate	consider
choice	consist
circle	Constitution

Diagnostic Sentences

151–175

1. During the **conversation,** he offered good **counsel** about the **contract** but failed to **convince** us to **continue** with the work.
2. The **cottage** in the **country** will **contain** a long work **counter** with **copper** trim.
3. A **coward** considers his lack of **courage** in **dangerous** situations a **cruel curse.**
4. In the **course** of repairing the **damage** to the **dairy** plant, the **crew** found a **cradle** used in colonial days.
5. The **daily** market **curve** showed that the **custom curtain** business was not worth a **crumb.**

176–200

1. Unless you can **declare** war on the **delight** offered by **dessert,** you need not **describe** how you are going on a **diet.**
2. His **decision** to make a **declaration** that the **deal** had driven him into **debt** would **deceive** no one.
3. The **delegate** claimed that **defeat** faced **democracy** if we allowed economy to **destroy** our **defense** plans.
4. After the train had left the **depot,** the old **democrat** looked over the **deed** he had to **deliver** when he reached his **destination.**
5. I must **differ** with the **dictionary** because this **diamond** is a **descendant** of those used to **decorate** the royal crown.

Average List Continued

151–175	176–200
contain	deal
continue	debt
contract	deceive
conversation	decision
convince	declaration
copper	declare
cottage	decorate
counsel	deed
counter	defeat
country	defense
courage	delegate
course	delight
coward	deliver
cradle	democracy
crew	democrat
cruel	depot
crumb	descendant
curse	describe
curtain	dessert
curve	destination
custom	destroy
daily	diamond
dairy	dictionary
damage	diet
dangerous	differ

Diagnostic Sentences

201–225

1. As the **duke** paused on his way **downstairs,** he moved **easily** and looked like an **eagle** standing at the **edge** of a cliff, seeking some **diversion.**
2. If she did **discover** that the **domestic** was **dishonest,** she would have to **discuss** it with the **district** officer.
3. It was **difficult** to **discharge** the **director** because he was so **earnest** and **eager** to please.
4. No **doubt** few would **disagree** that we had to **educate** every **druggist** in the new treatment of the **disease.**
5. In due time, he began to **dream,** and it seemed that his **direct double** was coming in his **direction.**

226–250

1. To avoid an **error,** enclose the **employment** slip in an **envelope** and mail it to your employer.
2. The **engineer** worked with **enthusiasm** and seemed to **enjoy** his **effort** to connect the **elevator** to the **electricity** supply.
3. **Everybody** was told **eventually** to be **especially** careful to make an **exact** drawing of the **engine** and to try not to use an **eraser.**
4. Before you **entertain,** try to **engage** someone to **embroider** the tablecloth to **establish** the **effect** of handmade linen.
5. After the **election,** he decided to **escape** to **Europe** to inspect the new **electric** plants of the British **Empire.**

Average List Continued

201–225	226–250
difficult	effect
direct	effort
direction	election
director	electric
disagree	electricity
discharge	elevator
discover	embroider
discuss	empire
disease	employment
dishonest	engage
district	engine
diversion	engineer
domestic	enjoy
double	entertain
doubt	enthusiasm
downstairs	envelope
dream	eraser
druggist	error
duke	escape
eager	especially
eagle	establish
earnest	Europe
easily	eventually
edge	everybody
educate	exact

Diagnostic Sentences

251–275

1. In our **experience,** this is just an **excuse** to **exchange** the **faucet** at our **expense.**
2. It was an **extreme example** of a **female** hat, with a long **feather** and what seemed like a **feast** of fruits.
3. The **failure** of his appeal to the **federal** courts meant that the state would **execute** the **famous** prisoner without further **examination.**
4. Why doesn't the examiner **explain** to that **fellow** that he should become **familiar** with the **export** laws?
5. A **fault** of those who cannot **fasten** themselves to some **faith** is that they tend to **exaggerate** the **external** expression of their doubts.

276–300

1. The **foreman** of the **freight** department found it hard to resist **frequent** dishes of **fried** fish.
2. Unless you wear a **flannel** shirt, you will **freeze** during the **flight** because it may be your bad **fortune** to run into some **fierce** winds.
3. On the **following** day, the **funeral** was held for the lonely **figure** who had **frozen** to death near the **fountain.**
4. **Finally,** the old **florist** came **forth** and asked the **feminine** customer to **forgive** him for failing in his **function.**
5. A country built on a **firm foundation** of **freedom** tries to be **friendly** but does not **frighten** easily if rejected.

Average List Continued

251–275	276–300
exaggerate	feminine
examination	fierce
example	figure
exchange	finally
excuse	firm
execute	flannel
expense	flight
experience	florist
explain	following
export	foreman
expression	forgive
external	forth
extreme	fortune
failure	foundation
faith	fountain
familiar	freedom
famous	freeze
fasten	freight
faucet	frequent
fault	fried
feast	friendly
feather	frighten
federal	frozen
fellow	function
female	funeral

Diagnostic Sentences

301–325

1. The **garment** found in the **garage** was covered with **generous** smears of **grease** and smelled of **gasoline.**
2. **Furthermore,** to **furnish** the art **gallery** with **genuine** old **furniture** is a job for the **governor.**
3. With a **gentle** smile, the lady in the blue **gown** goes toward the door to **greet** the tall **gentleman.**
4. It was **funny** to see the **goose** looking at a **geography** book like a **general** making **future** plans over a map.
5. In great **fury,** Peters rushed out to see who had thrown **garbage** into the **furnace,** but the culprit was **gone** and further search was useless.

326–350

1. In the **hygiene** class, we were told, however, that eating only **hominy** grits with **honey** could not keep one **healthy.**
2. As he took the **harness** off the handsome horse, his hearty **hello** showed his **happiness** that the **harvest** was complete without a **headache.**
3. The **guard** asked for the **honor** to **guide** the **guest** to the **history** classes where he could **guarantee** good lessons.
4. So great were the **honest grief** and **guilt** of the **heroine** that she seemed to be heading for poor **health.**
5. From the **height** of his window, he threw the pot **handle** in a **hurry,** his **grievance** being that the dog would nightly howl at the **heaven** above.

Average List Continued

301–325	**326–350**
funny	grief
furnace	grievance
furnish	guarantee
furniture	guard
furthermore	guest
fury	guide
future	guilt
gallery	handle
garage	happiness
garbage	harness
garment	harvest
gasoline	headache
general	health
generous	healthy
gentle	heaven
gentleman	height
genuine	hello
geography	heroine
goes	history
gone	hominy
goose	honest
governor	honey
gown	honor
grease	hurry
greet	hygiene

Diagnostic Sentences

351–375

1. No **immigrant** need remain **ignorant** if he is **industrious** in his efforts to **inquire** and get **information** about his new land.
2. **Industry** and labor will hold an **important** meeting **immediately** and will **include** talk about an **ideal increase.**
3. To show his **independence,** the **industrial** leader refused to **imitate** the idea because it would **injure** his name.
4. We must stress the **importance** of confining certain insane types because **improvement** for them is **impossible,** and they may cause **injury** to someone.
5. In its **innocence,** youth is **impatient** to be **independent** and can **imagine** no need for the **influence** of older heads to **illustrate** how harmful this can be.

376–400

1. An **invitation** was sent to the agent to collect the second **installment** on the **insurance** for the crown **jewel** of the **kingdom.**
2. By ordering the **inspector** to **investigate** the quality of the canned **juice,** the **judge** showed a fine sense of **justice.**
3. Let me **introduce** Mr. Kent, whose **intention** during the **interview** is to **interpret** the **judicial** report.
4. After putting some **kerosene** into a **kettle,** the **janitor,** following the **instruction** sheet, poured it on the insect nest.
5. Our **journey** to the **internal** region is to remove the **jealousy** that has blown tempers as high as a **kite** over the issue of **irrigation.**

Average List Continued

351–375	376–400
ideal	inspector
ignorant	installment
illustrate	instruction
imagine	insurance
imitate	intention
immediately	internal
immigrant	interpret
impatient	interview
importance	introduce
important	investigate
impossible	invitation
improvement	irrigation
include	issue
increase	janitor
independence	jealousy
independent	jewel
industrial	journey
industrious	judge
industry	judicial
influence	juice
information	justice
injure	kerosene
injury	kettle
innocence	kingdom
inquire	kite

Diagnostic Sentences

401–425

1. To gain more **knowledge** for her **license** test as **librarian,** Sally attended every **lecture** at the **library.**
2. Label Tom a **liar,** if you will, but he said at **least** some cheese on **lettuce** leaves and glasses of **lemonade** were served at the **lawn** party.
3. The **lawyer** told the **leader** of the **legion** that new **legislation** made him **liable** for the actions of his group.
4. Under the **lantern** was a sign on the **laundry** door **knob,** and I saw I was at **liberty** to sign a **lease** for the building.
5. Besides scratching her **knuckle,** the **kitten** had put such a **knot** in the wool on the **leather** chair that no one could **knit** with it now.

426–450

1. A **manual** of **material** needed to **manufacture** the new **locomotive** was issued with the **machinery.**
2. The slight **maiden** taking her **marriage** vows with her **masculine** partner made a lovely picture before the **magistrate.**
3. **Madam,** this **luxury mattress** is sewed by special **machine,** and you can **lounge** on it as shown in the **magazine.**
4. It was **manifest** that the **lieutenant** could not **manage** his **liquor** because he acted as if he had been struck by **lightning.**
5. People with good **manners** would not **loiter** long at the **marble** staircase, for it was the **location** of the **liquid** refreshments.

Average List Continued

401–425	426–450
kitten	lieutenant
knit	lightning
knob	liquid
knot	liquor
knowledge	location
knuckle	locomotive
lantern	loiter
laundry	lounge
lawn	luxury
lawyer	machine
leader	machinery
lease	madam
least	magazine
leather	magistrate
lecture	maiden
legion	manage
legislation	manifest
lemonade	manners
lettuce	manual
liable	manufacture
liar	marble
liberty	marriage
librarian	masculine
library	material
license	mattress

Diagnostic Sentences

451—475

1. In his **message** to the group, the **minister** had to **mention** the **mortgage** on the **modest** church property.
2. The **mistress** of the **millinery** shop had made a **model** in the **modern mode.**
3. **Minus** the dew and **mold** on the ground, the **midnight** walk in the **meadow** would have left a wonderful **memory.**
4. With a **mighty** swing of his arm, the **miller** struck the **mechanic,** and soon every **merchant** on the street was watching the **mortal** combat.
5. A **messenger** was sent by the **military** governor of **Mexico** to ask for supplies of **molasses** and **mineral** spirits.

476—500

1. It seems to be in the **nature** of the **Negro** to have a **natural** sense of **musical movement.**
2. People of every **nationality** pass through the **narrow** entrance to New York harbor to escape the **neglect** of their **native** lands and seek **naturalization** here.
3. Her **neighbor** removed the **napkin** from the **mutton** stew and, seeing that a dead **mosquito** lay on top of it, said **nobody** should eat it.
4. The **naughty** boy was **mute** when the **neuter** gender was mentioned, and the teacher grabbed him by the **necktie** with **murder** in her eye.
5. Knowing the **nomination** would not come from a **neutral** source if he came late, Collins strained **nearly** every **muscle** to start the **motor.**

Average List Continued

451–475	476–500
meadow	mosquito
mechanic	motor
memory	movement
mention	murder
merchant	muscle
message	musical
messenger	mute
Mexico	mutton
midnight	napkin
mighty	narrow
military	nationality
miller	native
millinery	natural
mineral	naturalization
minister	nature
minus	naughty
mistress	nearly
mode	necktie
model	neglect
modern	Negro
modest	neighbor
molasses	neuter
mold	neutral
mortal	nobody
mortgage	nomination

Diagnostic Sentences

501–525

1. Please **notify** the **oculist** that I shall **obey** his request to come to his **office** as soon as I get **official** leave.
2. The **odor** of cooked **oatmeal** and an **onion** being fried in **olive** oil assailed his **nostrils**.
3. There was **objection** to the **occupation** of the **northern** lands, and he dared not **offend** public **opinion**.
4. The **nurse** took an **oath** before a **notary** that it would be her **obligation** to meet all rules with **obedience**.
5. It did not **occur** to him that it would be a **nuisance** to **occupy** the center of the boat until he had to **oblige** by taking an **oar**.

526–550

1. One **patron** in **particular** was ready to **oppose** the new **orchestra** unless it included an **organ**.
2. The city **ordinance** stated that the **penalty** for a **peddler** who bothered a **patient** would be the **payment** of a fine.
3. When he felt the **package** slipping out of his **palm**, he turned **pale** because neither **parent** would **pardon** him nor **overwhelm** him with kindness if he broke the vase.
4. He thought it **peculiar** that the **passport** of the **passenger** **opposite** him in the **parlor** car was being checked.
5. Unless your **partner** has booked **passage** on a fast boat, it will be an **otherwise** **ordinary** task to overtake him.

Average List Continued

501–525	526–550
northern	oppose
nostrils	opposite
notary	orchestra
notify	ordinance
nuisance	ordinary
nurse	organ
oar	otherwise
oath	overwhelm
oatmeal	package
obedience	pale
obey	palm
objection	pardon
obligation	parent
oblige	parlor
occupation	particular
occupy	partner
occur	passage
oculist	passenger
odor	passport
offend	patient
office	patron
official	payment
olive	peculiar
onion	peddler
opinion	penalty

Diagnostic Sentences

551–575

1. A **pleasant** moment at the **picnic** was the playing of a **popular piano** piece on the **phonograph.**
2. The **police** asked the **physician** to test the amount of **poison** put into the **pepper** eaten by the **porter.**
3. After the **poll,** every **plumber** in the union gave a **pledge** of ten **percent** of his wages for the **political** drive.
4. It was a **pleasure** to sit on the **porch** with a **pitcher** of lemonade before us, and have a **polite** talk on **politics.**
5. Temple refused to **perform** at his own **peril** unless a **photograph** were taken of a **portion** of the **plaster** wall that looked ready to fall out.

576–600

1. The **priest** was unable to **prevail** upon the **prince** to allow a **prayer** to be said for the **prisoner.**
2. It is **probable** that the department will **proclaim** new **postal** rates to **preserve** the **present** services.
3. If you **prefer** to **prepare** the mixture by the old **process, pour** some **powder** into a cup and then add water.
4. Send **postage,** and we will solve your **problem** of how to **practice** the dance **position** in **private.**
5. He had to **pretend** to be able to **produce** any results because he was eager to **procure** the **praise** of the **powerful** men.

Average List Continued

551–575	576–600
pepper	position
percent	postage
perform	postal
peril	pour
phonograph	powder
photograph	powerful
physician	practice
piano	praise
picnic	prayer
pitcher	prefer
plaster	prepare
pleasant	present
pleasure	preserve
pledge	pretend
plumber	prevail
poison	priest
police	prince
polite	prisoner
political	private
politics	probable
poll	problem
popular	process
porch	proclaim
porter	procure
portion	produce

Diagnostic Sentences

601–625

1. I **propose** that we serve **prune pudding** and **pumpkin** pie at the end of the **program.**
2. The **professor** agreed to **promote** the **pupil** when he would **prove** he could **pronounce** each word.
3. Every **property** deed had a **purple** stamp that the owner had to **purchase** as **proof** that a **proper** deal had been made.
4. To **protect** the public, the city will **prohibit** the sale of the **product** for a **profit,** and will **punish** offenders.
5. The **purpose** the legal **profession** had in wanting to **publish** the report was to **provide** a **prompt** answer to its critics.

626–650

1. With her **quantity** of **raven** hair, the **queen** was easy to **recognize** as she entered the **railroad** coach.
2. His refusal to **quarrel** about the **rake** showed that he was trying to **redeem** himself and forget his former **record** as a **rebel.**
3. On a **recent radio** program, a **rabbi** was asked to **recite** some prayers that had been found in an old **reader.**
4. She found a piece of **rabbit** fur of good **quality** in her **purse,** and thought it **queer** that she couldn't **recall** whose it was.
5. During the **recess,** Joe was **really quite** happy when he was offered some of the **raisin** cake that was lying on the kitchen **range.**

Average List Continued

601–625	626–650
product	purse
profession	quality
professor	quantity
profit	quarrel
program	queen
prohibit	queer
promote	quite
prompt	rabbi
pronounce	rabbit
proof	radio
proper	railroad
property	raisin
propose	rake
protect	range
prove	raven
provide	reader
prune	really
publish	rebel
pudding	recall
pumpkin	recent
punish	recess
pupil	recite
purchase	recognize
purple	record
purpose	redeem

Diagnostic Sentences

651–675

1. The **reporter** asked Father Crowley to **relate** how he had brought **religion** to that **remote region**.
2. A special drive was on to **request** every **regular Republican** voter who was a **resident** to **register** for the election.
3. It was a **relief** to learn that Summers, who was held in high **regard**, would be able to **represent** the **republic** even under the new **regulation**.
4. In moments of **repose**, people can **repent** their sins, **repair** their souls, **regain** their confidence, and **renew** their hope.
5. You must **resist** any desire to **repeat** your **reference** to the incident at the **resort**, even to a **relative**.

676–700

1. When the **retail** trade took a **rude** drop, the **salesman** knew sales would have to **rocket** to **restore** his old **salary**.
2. A platter of **roast** beef, a green **salad**, and a piece of **rye** bread caused the **sailor** to **salute** his host.
3. Hit by a **rough** blow with the **rubber** hose, the robber let out a **roar** that had the **rhythm** of a **rubbish** truck.
4. Before I **resume** my talk, I **respectfully** ask my **rival** to **reveal** why his firm sold **rotten** fruit to the hospitals.
5. **Review** the **sacrifice** it took to check the **revolt**, and you can see why this man must **retain** your respect.

Average List Continued

651–675

reference
regain
regard
region
register
regular
regulation
relate
relative
relief
religion
remote
renew
repair
repeat
repent
reporter
repose
represent
republic
Republican
request
resident
resist
resort

676–700

respectfully
restore
resume
retail
retain
reveal
review
revolt
rhythm
rival
roar
roast
rocket
rotten
rough
rubber
rubbish
rude
rye
sacrifice
sailor
salad
salary
salesman
salute

Diagnostic Sentences

701–725

1. In his **search** to **secure** a good **secretary**, he will **select** only one who is **serious** about her work.
2. The **servant** brought some **sausage** and eggs to the **senator**, and a **shallow saucer** of milk for his pet cat.
3. A **scream** had been heard at the **scene**, but evidence was **scarce** because everyone had been able to **scatter** before the police could **seize** a witness.
4. Because we want the **screen** over the **sewer** openings now, don't **scratch** your head like a **scholar** but get your **share** of the work done.
5. You may have to **settle** some **severe** differences of opinion before your **selection** for the post will **satisfy** the **Senate**.

726–750

1. Even the **shawl** gave little **shelter**, and when a **slight shiver** was followed by a **sneeze**, she went inside.
2. It is **simple** to **sharpen** the tool so that a **single** turn will cut a **smooth slice**.
3. **Somebody** must have given a **signal** to the **sheriff** who has just **shown** his **shield** and taken charge.
4. The **society** members were **sincere** when they said that his **signature** on the letter of resignation was a **source** of **sorrow** to them.
5. Kicking off a **slipper**, she watched the **soda** clerk in **sober silence** as he tried to **shovel** some ice cream into a plate.

Average List Continued

701–725	726–750
satisfy	sharpen
saucer	shawl
sausage	shelter
scarce	sheriff
scatter	shield
scene	shiver
scholar	shovel
scratch	shown
scream	signal
screen	signature
search	silence
secretary	simple
secure	sincere
seize	single
select	slice
selection	slight
Senate	slipper
senator	smooth
serious	sneeze
servant	sober
settle	society
severe	soda
sewer	somebody
shallow	sorrow
share	source

Diagnostic Sentences

751–775

1. As the old **statesman** rose on the **stage** to give his **speech**, we sang "The Star-**Spangled** Banner" with great **spirit**.
2. The retired **station** agent would sit in the town **square** and **spread** crumbs of **stale** bread for his **sparrow** friends.
3. At the **steam** table, I found the choice to be **steak**, **spinach** and corn, or **spare** ribs in a **special** sauce.
4. When the **speaker** made a **statement** about those who **sponge** on the state and **steal** public funds, some **spice** came into his talk.
5. A **splendid** appeal by the chairman broke the **steady** effort of the **standard** bearers of the **southern** group to form a **splinter** party.

776–800

1. All of a **sudden**, a shell ripped through a **steel** plate **structure** in the **stern** near the **steerage** and caused a **stir** in the engine room.
2. **Strife** had broken out above the **stream** where only **superior** land **strength** would **succeed** in turning back the enemy.
3. He tried to **stretch** his arm, but the **strange** pain in his **stomach** made it a **struggle** to **steer**.
4. By a stroke of luck, the **substitute** for the regular **stenographer** was such a **success** that Miss Webb had no need to **summon** help.
5. A **stripe** is in **style** this year, but we **suggest** that you **submit** a few more sketches on the **subject**.

Average List Continued

751–775	776–800
southern	steel
spangle	steer
spare	steerage
sparrow	stenographer
speaker	stern
special	stir
speech	stomach
spice	strange
spinach	stream
spirit	strength
splendid	stretch
splinter	strife
sponge	stripe
spread	structure
square	struggle
stage	style
stale	subject
standard	submit
statement	substitute
statesman	succeed
station	success
steady	sudden
steak	suggest
steal	summon
steam	superior

Diagnostic Sentences

801–825

1. To see the actor **swallow** the **sword** was a **surprise** to the **surgeon** who was once heard to **swear** it was impossible to do.
2. The **supply** company had a **terrible** trip through the **swamp** because one **swarm** of insects after another rose from its **surface.**
3. On a **tablet** in the old **temple,** someone with **talent** had outlined the **system** of worship under the **supreme** ruler.
4. If you want the **support** of the chief **teller,** don't lose your **temper** if he refuses to **telegraph** the money to the **sweater** concern.
5. I **suppose** it wasn't odd in the summer to see a man sitting in front of a **tenement, suspenders** down, shirt **tail** out, and **sweat** pouring from his brow.

826–850

1. The **tiger** has been a **thorn** in the sides of the people of that **territory** and has struck **terror** in the hearts of the timid.
2. A distant clap of **thunder** seemed to **threaten** rain, which we **thought** would relieve the **thirst** of the crops **throughout** the area.
3. The **thief** tried to escape by the **toilet** window but met with total defeat when he slipped on a **thimble,** gashed his **thigh,** and injured his **throat.**
4. A little **tomato** juice, a piece of **toast,** and a pipeful of **tobacco** were enough of a **tonic** to **tide** him over until he could entirely **throttle** his hunger pangs at supper.
5. Pointing with his **thumb** toward the tidy little house, he spoke of a **token** deposit before **title** and **therefore** asked for a check.

Average List Continued

801–825	826–850
supply	territory
support	terror
suppose	therefore
supreme	thief
surface	thigh
surgeon	thimble
surprise	thirst
suspenders	thorn
swallow	thought
swamp	threaten
swarm	throat
swear	throttle
sweat	throughout
sweater	thumb
sword	thunder
system	tide
tablet	tidy
tail	tiger
talent	title
telegraph	toast
teller	tobacco
temper	toilet
temple	token
tenement	tomato
terrible	tonic

Diagnostic Sentences

851–875

1. A **trailer** truck had hit a **trolley,** and police were **unable** to clear up **traffic** in the **tunnel** for an hour.
2. The tribe had sent the **trustee** a **transcript** of an original native **tune** as a **tribute** to his good **treatment** of their **trophy.**
3. If you twist some plastic **twine** around that **ugly tube,** you can use it as a **towel** bar.
4. Because no **trace** of the **typist** could be found, it was **transparent** that the **treasurer** himself would have to use the **typewriter** to complete the stock **transfer** form.
5. On his return from a **tough** treasure hunt, the **traveler** ate the **turkey** gladly, but refused the cooked **turnip.**

876–900

1. Not knowing it was **unlawful** to **unbutton** his **uniform,** the **unfortunate** cadet was caught and sent **upstairs.**
2. Although a bit **unusual,** the **university** will **undertake** to **unite** the **union** members by offering a course in labor problems.
3. The **urge** to be **useful** is a **universal** trait, and people are **unhappy** if old age or illness makes them feel **useless.**
4. For some **unknown** reason, a boy climbed **upward** to an **unfurnished** room in the **upper** story and was **unseen** by us.
5. **Unlike** his **unhealthy** brother, Jim will find the **uneven, untried** climate harmless, **unless** we are mistaken.

Average List Continued

851–875	876–900
tough	unbutton
towel	undertake
trace	uneven
traffic	unfortunate
trailer	unfurnished
transcript	unhappy
transfer	unhealthy
transparent	uniform
traveler	union
treasurer	unite
treatment	universal
tribute	university
trolley	unknown
trophy	unlawful
trustee	unless
tube	unlike
tune	unseen
tunnel	untried
turkey	unusual
turnip	upper
twine	upstairs
typewriter	upward
typist	urge
ugly	useful
unable	useless

Diagnostic Sentences

901–925

1. The **usher** tried in **vain** to reach the **vacant** seat, but to his **utter** disgust the small man was the **victor** in the race.
2. **Veto** that bill and you will **vex** everyone in the **valley,** who will consider it a **victory** for the forces of **vice.**
3. On her **vacation,** she loved to walk in the **vale** where a **variety** of **valuable** orchids were everywhere in **view.**
4. **Various** seasonings, including **vanilla,** were added to the **veal** cooking in the **utensil,** whose great **value** was its **vapor** seal.
5. Every **vein** of the captain of the **vessel** stood out as he tried his **utmost** to **verify** the report that he had been the **victim** of a plot.

926–950

1. So **weak** had her voyage through the **vocabulary** lists made the **weary** girl that all she could do was **wail** and **weep.**
2. He showed a **visible** wealth of talent with the **violin,** and it would be a **waste** not to make playing it his **vocation.**
3. The **waiter** had put such a **volume** of vinegar in the dish that the **vile** taste made the diner **vomit.**
4. At the **wedding** of the **wealthy** broker, a **watchman** was hired to keep the grounds **void** of intruders who might **wander** in.
5. With a look of **virtue** on his face, the **warden** announced with **vigor** that he had found the **weapon** in a **violet** bed.

Average List Continued

901–925	926–950
usher	vigor
utensil	vile
utmost	vinegar
utter	violet
vacant	violin
vacation	virtue
vain	visible
vale	vocabulary
valley	vocation
valuable	void
value	volume
vanilla	vomit
vapor	voyage
variety	wail
various	waiter
veal	wander
vein	warden
verify	waste
vessel	watchman
veto	weak
vex	wealthy
vice	weapon
victim	weary
victory	wedding
view	weep

Diagnostic Sentences

951–975

1. We heard the **witness whisper** to the **widow** that he would **withdraw** from the case **whether** or not she was **willing.**
2. **Wheat** was sent by the **western** world **wherever** and **whenever** it could serve the **welfare** of the poor.
3. **Whatever** the **wholesale** price of the **wheelbarrow** is, be sure to get the proper **width** and a rubber **wheel.**
4. **Whence** the wine barrel had come was beyond his **wisdom,** but the **weight** of it made him pause to wipe his brow.
5. The **whistle** of the boy coming down from the **willow** tree **wholly** stopped when the **wicked** old farmer struck him with a **wire whip.**

976–1000

1. **You're** right when you say that the **youth** will be a good worker because he wants **worse** than ever to end the **woe** of unemployment.
2. The **youngster** did no more than **wrench** his **wrist,** but his main **worry** was how to **worm** his way out of the **wreck** of the **yacht.**
3. His career reached the **zenith** when his **wonderful** carving of a **wooden zebra** was judged **worthy** of the grand prize.
4. I wouldn't mind if yonder **wretch** would only **yawn** when I play the **zither,** but the **worst** of it is he snores, too.
5. Trying to take the **yeast** stain out of her **woolen wrap,** all she did was **wound** herself on the **zipper.**

Average List Continued

951–975	976–1000
weight	woe
welfare	wonderful
western	wooden
whatever	woolen
wheat	worm
wheel	worry
wheelbarrow	worse
whence	worst
whenever	worthy
wherever	wound
whether	wrap
whip	wreck
whisper	wrench
whistle	wretch
wholesale	wrist
wholly	yacht
wicked	yawn
widow	yeast
width	youngster
willing	you're
willow	youth
wire	zebra
wisdom	zenith
withdraw	zipper
witness	zither

Thirty-Day Trial List

Diagnostic Sentences

1–20

1. A **capacity** crowd watched the **American** team win the **benefit basketball** game.
2. With the **cooperation** of the salesman, who showed her the catalog, she was able to buy some **acceptable clothes.**
3. Much **criticism** was directed against the **committee** for using its **authority** without a legal **basis.**
4. No one in good **conscience** would issue a **bulletin** without first trying to **ascertain** the **bearing** it would have on the **casualty** figures.
5. Your **courtesy** in offering to **accommodate** my **acquaintance** will be **cordially** repaid.

21–40

1. A **guardian** will be **duly** named to keep **definite** control over **financial** matters.
2. By some **miracle,** the **exhausted** boys reached the **dormitory** before their **mischief** was discovered.
3. In the **judgment** of the dealer, it would be an **excellent edition** to add to his collection of classic **literature.**
4. The chief **executive** of the **government** made an **extraordinary farewell** address.
5. We will not **interrupt** the building of the **extension** if we can **determine** the **existence** of a proper permit.

Thirty-Day Trial

1–20	21–40
acceptable	definite
accommodate	determine
acquaintance	dormitory
American	duly
ascertain	edition
authority	excellent
basis	executive
basketball	exhausted
bearing	existence
benefit	extension
bulletin	extraordinary
capacity	farewell
casualty	financial
clothes	government
committee	guardian
conscience	interrupt
cooperation	judgment
cordially	literature
courtesy	miracle
criticism	mischief

Diagnostic Sentences

Thirty-Day Trial Continued

41–60

1. **Undoubtedly,** the **monarchy** would not return because a **recommendation** had been made to exile the **sovereign.**
2. It will be **necessary** for me to get a **quantity** of slides to meet a **requirement** of the **zoology** class.
3. I heard one **peasant murmur** that the **warrant** for the arrest of the official should contain a **treason** charge.
4. Have the good **sense** on this **occasion** to take a **thorough** grasp of the **opportunity.**
5. Our **original** plan was to sign for a **partial** period **prior** to any **permanent** arrangement.

Review of FSA Rule

1–20

1. It **occurred** to us that we had **omitted** evidence that **merited** attention because it could lead to **acquittal.**
2. The board **canceled** the contract for the new **propeller** when the manufacturer **admitted** he had **exceeded** the specifications.
3. It was **regrettable** that some were **profiting** from the **allotted** food shipments and **forgetting** their pledge to distribute at cost.
4. Out of **deference,** we **telegramed** our congratulations after the committee **conferred** and agreed to honor the **commitment.**
5. In the **skinning** operation, it was found **preferable** to use the new drying process because the furs **benefited** and **recurring** problems of shrinkage were avoided.

*Thirty-Day Trial
Continued*

*Review of
FSA Rule*

41–60

1–20

monarchy	acquittal
murmur	admitted
necessary	allotted
occasion	benefited
opportunity	canceled
original	commitment
partial	conferred
peasant	deference
permanent	exceeded
prior	forgetting
quantity	merited
recommendation	occurred
requirement	omitted
sense	preferable
sovereign	profiting
thorough	propeller
treason	recurring
undoubtedly	regrettable
warrant	skinning
zoology	telegramed

Diagnostic Sentences

1–25

1. **Accordingly,** we will **adjourn** this case until you bring a signed **affidavit** from your **accountant** that the **agreement** existed.
2. No **adjective** could describe his **agony** as he knelt in the **aisle** to ask the **Almighty** for an **abatement** of his sorrow.
3. An **abundance** of **alcohol** always would **affect** him with an air of abandon, speech full of **alliteration,** and a desire for **adventure.**
4. The **acknowledgment** that use of the **alloy** would be **all right** and in **accordance** with plans was **accidentally** mislaid.
5. Man will not **accustom** himself to letting others **abridge** his freedom, however much they seek to **achieve** his **admiration** by speaking **affectionately** of justice.

26–50

1. When the **altos** joined in the **ancient** song, our **appreciation** and **applause** mounted because the chorus sounded **altogether** like a group of **angels.**
2. **Apparently,** the **ambassador** had sought the arrangement of an **appropriation** for his **area.**
3. From the **appearance** of things, the operation for **appendicitis** could not be performed on the **arctic** explorer because no **antiseptic** or **anesthesia** was **anywhere** to be found.
4. The **ambitious architect** was glad to **announce** that his **apparatus** had been **approved** for the **annual** show.
5. **Approximately** a dozen tutors had tried vainly from every **angle** to get Roger to appreciate his **ancestors,** but he remained aloof.

Advanced List

1–25	26–50
abatement	altogether
abridge	altos
abundance	ambassador
accidentally	ambitious
accordance	ancestors
accordingly	ancient
accountant	anesthesia
accustom	angels
achieve	angle
acknowledgment	announce
adjective	annual
adjourn	antiseptic
admiration	anywhere
adventure	apparatus
affect	apparently
affectionately	appearance
affidavit	appendicitis
agony	applause
agreement	appreciation
aisle	appropriation
alcohol	approved
alliteration	approximately
alloy	architect
all right	arctic
Almighty	area

Diagnostic Sentences

51–75

1. A large **audience** came to the **balcony** of the **armory** to watch the **banquet** being given for the star **athlete.**
2. On the **average,** he kept ten sacks of **barley available** in his **basement** for the **assistance** of the poor.
3. I shall **assign** an **attendant** to tell the author not to **ascend** the platform before the people **assemble** for the **barbecue.**
4. The **ballistics** expert seemed to **assume** it would **astonish** us to learn of the **barbarous** treatment even babies were given after the village was **attacked.**
5. Her **beauty** could so **attract** men that they were forever **attaching** themselves, although she kept **assuring** them they would go into **bankruptcy** buying her presents.

76–100

1. On her **blouse** she wore two **cameos** which had **bronze** clips and **butterfly** designs in **brilliant** colors.
2. The **burglar** did not **beware** of the dog at the **boundary** of the estate, but one **bestial** growl sent him up the **bough** of a tree.
3. In the **beginning** it was our **belief** that the **bricklayer** had gone over our **budget** by a hair's **breadth.**
4. The **brokerage** firm knew that no one would **boycott** a party where besides sandwiches there was a cool **beverage bubbling** in a large **bucket.**
5. At the **burial,** someone **brought** a **bugle** to his lips, as the captain, holding the **bridle** of his horse, stood with head bowed under his **burden** of grief.

Advanced List Continued

51–75	76–100
armory	beginning
ascend	belief
assemble	bestial
assign	beverage
assistance	beware
assume	blouse
assuring	bough
astonish	boundary
athlete	boycott
attaching	breadth
attacked	bricklayer
attendant	bridle
attract	brilliant
audience	brokerage
available	bronze
average	brought
balcony	bubbling
ballistics	bucket
bankruptcy	budget
banquet	bugle
barbarous	burden
barbecue	burglar
barley	burial
basement	butterfly
beauty	cameos

Diagnostic Sentences

101–125

1. The **ceremony** was in **celebration** of the end of the **campaign** that had carried the **champion** to a new **challenge** in his **career.**
2. **Canoeing** down the river, Tom pulled his **camera** out of its **canvas** cover so that he could **capture** the lovely sight of the distant **cathedral.**
3. When the **cargoes** arrived at the **cannery,** the **celery** and **cauliflower** crates were unloaded, but the **cantaloupe** shipment was sent back.
4. As the **cavalry** swept past the **cemetery** toward the **captive** company, the roar of the **cannon** did not **cease.**
5. From its office in the **capitol,** the **census** bureau announced a new **canvass** of the **changeable** population if **capable** workers could be found.

126–150

1. In the **chapel,** the **community** **choir** sang several **Christian** hymns in **commendable** fashion.
2. By **comparison,** the **cobbler** could **claim** more **chargeable** accounts than the **clothier.**
3. The **commission** sent a **circular** through the **colony,** warning that **chauvinism** had always been a threat to **civilization.**
4. According to the report of the **chemist,** someone with **coarse** **chestnut** hair has **committed** the crime against the **colonist.**
5. A **communication** from the **circus** manager said that under no **circumstances** would the **combination** dive be permitted from the top of the **column.**

Advanced List Continued

101–125	126–150
camera	chapel
campaign	chargeable
cannery	chauvinism
cannon	chemist
canoeing	chestnut
cantaloupe	choir
canvas	Christian
canvass	circular
capable	circumstances
capitol	circus
captive	civilization
career	claim
cargoes	clothier
cathedral	coarse
cauliflower	cobbler
cavalry	colonist
cease	colony
celebration	column
celery	combination
cemetery	commendable
census	commission
ceremony	committed
challenge	communication
champion	community
changeable	comparison

Diagnostic Sentences

151–175

1. **Confidence** in his **compass** made him **completely** sure he would avoid **confusion** even if he went a **considerable** way into the woods on his **conservation** trip.
2. If neither side will **concede** ground in the matter of **compensation,** you will **compel** me to **conclude** the **conference.**
3. He had to **confess** that he had cheated in the class **competition,** and it was small **consolation** that his **comrade** did not **condemn** him.
4. **Consequently,** after the **compilation** of the facts, everyone could **comprehend** why an effort was made to **conceal** their **connection** with the senator.
5. Although he would try to construct a new **composition** for the **complexion** cream, he was **conscious** of the **consequence** of failure.

176–200

1. At the **convention,** one doctor told a **credible** story of how he had **created** a **continuous** check on the **contagious** disease by setting up a **controlled** group.
2. In a **contemptible** effort to avoid **criminal** charges, the **corrupt controller** of the **corporation** left town.
3. Several countries on the **continent** organized a **council** in order to **consult** with one another about the proper **conveyance** of defense plans.
4. Only the **continual** sound of a **cricket** disturbed the strange **creature** as he scrawled a bit of **correspondence** with a large **crayon.**
5. **Contrary** to our expectations, the **contractor** had shown a **cordial** interest in our **convenience** by making the porch **convertible** to an all-year room.

Advanced List Continued

151–175	176–200
compass	consult
compel	contagious
compensation	contemptible
competition	continent
compilation	continual
completely	continuous
complexion	contractor
composition	contrary
comprehend	controlled
comrade	controller
conceal	convenience
concede	convention
conclude	convertible
condemn	conveyance
conference	cordial
confess	corporation
confidence	correspondence
confusion	corrupt
connection	council
conscious	crayon
consequence	created
consequently	creature
conservation	credible
considerable	cricket
consolation	criminal

Diagnostic Sentences

201–225

1. The **delicate** care with which the nurse placed a **cushion** behind the **delirious cripple** seemed to be a **denial** of her reputation for **cruelty.**
2. These **dahlia** seeds will give **delightful** flowers, and if you **cultivate** the **cucumber** patch, you will have a **delicious** addition to your summer menu.
3. It was **curious** to see how the **decrease** of supplies in the **cupboard** had made her **dependent** on the **delivery** service.
4. In his **deposition** before the judge, Mr. Cole pointed out the **degree** to which the once **dependable** market had fallen into a **current decline.**
5. A **cursory** glance at the **dense** growth made him decide to **defy** the **decree** of his landscaper not to use the grass cutter.

226–250

1. From the **description** of the footprints, the **detective** believed that the **difference** in **depth** between the two was **destined** to solve the case.
2. He would **derive** more benefit if he were to **deprive** himself rather than **devour** everything in sight and have **difficulty** later trying to digest the food.
3. The **dilemma** he faced was the need to **devote** full time to the **development** of a new **design** for the **device** that would trap the agent of the **dictator.**
4. In the **directory** was the address of her **despised** relative, but **dignity** would not allow one to **descend** so low as to visit the **disagreeable** man.
5. **Diphtheria** in this **desolate** area would bring **destruction** and **despair** unless **desperate** efforts were made to fight it.

Advanced List Continued

201–225	**226–250**
cripple	deprive
cruelty	depth
cucumber	derive
cultivate	descend
cupboard	description
curious	design
current	desolate
cursory	despair
cushion	desperate
dahlia	despised
decline	destined
decrease	destruction
decree	detective
defy	development
degree	device
delicate	devote
delicious	devour
delightful	dictator
delirious	difference
delivery	difficulty
denial	dignity
dense	dilemma
dependable	diphtheria
dependent	directory
deposition	disagreeable

Diagnostic Sentences

251–275

1. Her **distress** did not **disturb** those who could **distinguish** real pain and **dismiss** this as a mood that would soon **disappear**.
2. I **dissent** because I am **disappointed** at your **discontent**, and I **disapprove** your **distinct** effort to **discourage** the others.
3. To **disobey** would be **disastrous**, but there was no way to **dissolve** the **dispute** without meeting with his **displeasure**.
4. We can **dispose** of the goods on display, although it's a **disgrace** to sell such **divine** dresses so low, even at a **discount**.
5. A **discovery** was made in the **dispensary** that certain **distinctive** markings helped remove the **disguise** from the odd skin **disorder**.

276–300

1. From his **duffel** bag he took the plan that showed how the **electronic** system would **duplicate** colors without need of **dyeing** the **elegant** cloth.
2. Hardly had the **echoes** of her **doubtful** past faded from the **divorce** trial when the **dreadful** news arrived that she had **drowned** herself.
3. The **educator** called the attention of the **editor** to the **doctrine** that an unstable **economy** will create **division** among the people.
4. When the **draftsman** **edited** the report of the **electrician**, he suggested an **elementary** way to make the estimate **divisible** into a unit price.
5. Nothing short of an **earthquake** will move **drowsy** donkeys, and it **doesn't** seem strange that sometimes their drivers would be **elated** if one came along.

Advanced List Continued

251–275	276–300
disappear	divisible
disappointed	division
disapprove	divorce
disastrous	doctrine
discontent	doesn't
discount	donkeys
discourage	doubtful
discovery	draftsman
disgrace	dreadful
disguise	drowned
dismiss	drowsy
disobey	duffel
disorder	duplicate
dispensary	dyeing
displeasure	earthquake
dispose	echocs
dispute	economy
dissent	edited
dissolve	editor
distinct	educator
distinctive	elated
distinguish	electrician
distress	electronic
disturb	elegant
divine	elementary

Diagnostic Sentences

301–325

1. Your rescue of the leader from his **encounter** with the **enormous elephant** will **entitle** you to his **eternal** thanks.
2. Having lost the **esteem** of the **emperor,** Tito would now have to **emigrate elsewhere,** but he was not **equipped** for travel.
3. It was not easy for the **engraver** to **estimate** the cost of **enlarging** the **emblem** because of the **erasure** in the plan.
4. Billy would **embrace** the chance to run an **errand, especially** because mother would soon **encourage** him to supply **entertainment** for the guests on the piano.
5. In the **emergency,** one **employee** turned his **energy** upon the equipment in a loyal **endeavor** to repair it before the flow of **ether** stopped.

326–350

1. **Everyone** was **exhausted** by the **excess** of weeping at the news that Carlos had been **exiled** and would be **expatriated** for ten years.
2. One **explanation** of the failure of the **exclusive fashion everywhere** was its **exorbitant** price.
3. **Evidence** that the trip was over would **exhilarate** the **faithful** members of the **expedition** and make them cry out in **exultation.**
4. The **exhibit** would allow no **exception,** and if he dared **exceed** the limits of design, he would expose himself to being **expelled** for trying to **exploit** the regulations.
5. To **exclaim** about a threat of **famine** would **excite** the people and cause them to **explore** why other lands should **excel** theirs.

Advanced List Continued

301–325	326–350
elephant	everyone
elsewhere	everywhere
emblem	evidence
embrace	exceed
emergency	excel
emigrate	exception
emperor	excess
employee	excite
encounter	exclaim
encourage	exclusive
endeavor	exhausted
energy	exhibit
engraver	exhilarate
enlarging	exiled
enormous	exorbitant
entertainment	expatriated
entitle	expedition
equipped	expelled
erasure	explanation
errand	exploit
especially	explore
esteem	exultation
estimate	faithful
eternal	famine
ether	fashion

Diagnostic Sentences

351–375

1. A slight flutter of his **feeble** hand showed that the **forcible** feeding was having a favorable effect on what had seemed a **fatal** illness.
2. Our **foremost** regret was that we had to forsake this **fertile** land where fruits of wonderful **flavor** could **flourish** all year and plants would multiply by **fission.**
3. A **feature** of the **festival** was the showing of a **film** of the **fiery** singer who was a **favorite** of the **feminist** group.
4. It would not be **feasible** to market the **fluid fertilizer** unless they were **fortunate** in getting someone to **finance** the project and act as a **fiduciary.**
5. **Fidelity** is a **fixture** in marriage and tends to **forge** happiness for all but the **frivolous** who **flatter** themselves on being different.

376–400

1. At first, the **furrier** would **frown** and then become **furious** at his **futility** in learning **fundamental grammar.**
2. The **glitter** in the **gorgeous** hair of the **gracious** actress made her look like a **glorious** and **glamorous goddess** in all her **grandeur.**
3. To **fulfill** his promise to rid the grounds of every **grasshopper,** the gardener made **gradual** use of a fuel oil spray.
4. He was **fully** prepared to swear it was the **gospel** truth that he had seen a **ghost** wearing **goggles galloping** by on a horse.
5. Every **generation** in the family seemed to graduate a **glazier** who was a **genius** at creating graceful figures in blown glass.

Advanced List Continued

351–375	376–400
fatal	frown
favorite	fulfill
feasible	fully
feature	fundamental
feeble	furious
feminist	furrier
fertile	futility
fertilizer	galloping
festival	generation
fidelity	genius
fiduciary	ghost
fiery	glamorous
film	glazier
finance	glitter
fission	glorious
fixture	goddess
flatter	goggles
flavor	gorgeous
flourish	gospel
fluid	graceful
forcible	gracious
foremost	gradual
forge	grammar
fortunate	grandeur
frivolous	grasshopper

Diagnostic Sentences

401–425

1. The youthful **heir** was **grateful** for the way his **haughty guardian** was **handling** the affairs of the estate.
2. **Hereafter,** before I buy a tool to check the **growth** of the **hedge,** the **hardware** store will have to **guarantee** it.
3. Paul felt **guilty** about his **hatred** for the **greedy** old man and could hardly allow him to lie helpless in the gutter.
4. While I may **groan** about it, I **hereby** give you my word that **henceforth** I shall **heartily** welcome the work at the **gymnasium,** whatever the **hazard.**
5. Don't **grieve** over his loss of the **guitar** but **hasten** to express **gratitude** over the removal of your main **grievance** about his lack of **harmony.**

426–450

1. **Hurrah** for the humble **hoe,** which destroys the **immunity** enjoyed by the robbers of **honey.**
2. **Herewith** is an example of how this **idol** of the **household** listeners appeals to the **illiterate** who cannot see his **hypocrisy.**
3. In deep, **hollow** tones, the organ poured forth the **immortal hymn** of man's **heroic** struggle against the **horrible** forces of evil.
4. Anything blocking the **hexagon** sign on the **horizon** is a **hindrance** on a **highway** and should be removed **immediately** before it produces the **horror** of a crash.
5. Your **ignorance** about animals is beyond **imagination,** but come hither, and I shall tell you all about this **immense hippopotamus, heretofore** unknown to you.

Advanced List Continued

401–425	426–450
grateful	heretofore
gratitude	herewith
greedy	heroic
grievance	hexagon
grieve	highway
groan	hindrance
growth	hippopotamus
guarantee	hoe
guardian	hollow
guilty	honey
guitar	horizon
gymnasium	horrible
handling	horror
hardware	household
harmony	hurrah
hasten	hymn
hatred	hypocrisy
haughty	idol
hazard	ignorance
heartily	illiterate
hedge	imagination
heir	immediately
henceforth	immense
hereafter	immortal
hereby	immunity

Diagnostic Sentences

451–475

1. The **infinite** faith every **inhabitant** had in the **imperial** ruler's wisdom seemed to **indicate** that no one could **induce** them to revolt.
2. If you dare impose an **inferior instrument** on the artist, you will not only **inconvenience** him but arouse his **indignation**.
3. My **initial impression** of that **individual** served only to **inspire** an **instant** dislike for him.
4. At his **inauguration,** he spoke with **intelligence** of an **indivisible** nation and attacked by **innuendo** those who would fight **integration** in every **institution**.
5. Further **inquiry** showed that this was one **instance** where one could inherit a tendency that would **incline** him toward **indigestion** and require an **inoculation**.

476–500

1. In **league** with the old **knight,** Fenton worked out an invention that used an **invisible laser** beam to destroy ships rounding the **isthmus**.
2. The **legislature** made it a crime for any jeweler to sell without an **invoice,** and whether or not he could **justify** it was deemed **irrelevant**.
3. In the **interior** of her handbag was discovered the **intimate** little **ivory** figure that the **laundress** had found **irresistible**.
4. Attempts to **inveigle** a customer into buying a poorly labeled bottle of **iodine** will not **kindle** much **laughter** in a **laboratory**.
5. **Irregular jewelry** purchases by the **jockey** forced the board to **intercede** and turn him over to the **jurisdiction** of the courts.

Advanced List Continued

451–475	476–500
imperial	intercede
impression	interior
inauguration	intimate
incline	inveigle
inconvenience	invisible
indicate	invoice
indigestion	iodine
indignation	irregular
individual	irrelevant
indivisible	irresistible
induce	isthmus
inferior	ivory
infinite	jewelry
inhabitant	jockey
initial	jurisdiction
innuendo	justify
inoculation	kindle
inquiry	knight
inspire	labeled
instance	laboratory
instant	laser
institution	laughter
instrument	laundress
integration	league
intelligence	legislature

Diagnostic Sentences

501–525

1. **Maybe mama** wanted a **manicure** because she wished to look like the **majority** when she went for her **literacy** test.
2. The **lonely, majestic** figure walked up the **macadam** road toward the **magnificent mausoleum.**
3. Keep this **lively** book on your **mantel** because it is good reading and can **likewise lighten** your **leisure** moments.
4. Her **Majesty** found the **mansion** so **lonesome** that she would loose a wail like a caged **lunatic** whenever she suspected the **loyalty** of those who deserted her.
5. In the **meantime,** he learned that even a **mature** man would have to be built like a **longshoreman** to **maintain** the **lodge** all year.

526–550

1. The **medium** used a **metaphor** to describe her new method, by which she could, with a **mere** wave of her hand, **mesmerize** anyone who gave her **moderate** attention.
2. When the child had the **misfortune** to contract the **measles,** the **midwife** became **miserable** and lost all signs of **mirth.**
3. His misery mounted when he saw in the **mirror** that the **mischievous** driver had fixed the **meter** to record extra **mileage.**
4. A **memorandum** regarding the melon shipment pointed out that the **merchandise** had a **mixture** of quality and did not meet **minimum** standards.
5. **Meanwhile,** as the sad melody was played, he stood **midst** the crowd, wishing to **mingle** with those who had come to the **memorial** services for the **militant** leader who had tried to **mediate** the **missile** disagreement.

Advanced List Continued

501–525	526–550
leisure	meanwhile
lighten	measles
likewise	mediate
literacy	medium
lively	memorandum
lodge	memorial
lonely	merchandise
lonesome	mere
longshoreman	mesmerize
loyalty	metaphor
lunatic	meter
macadam	midst
magnificent	midwife
maintain	mileage
majestic	militant
majesty	mingle
majority	minimum
mama	mirror
manicure	mirth
mansion	mischievous
mantel	miserable
mature	misfortune
mausoleum	missile
maybe	mixture
meantime	moderate

Diagnostic Sentences

551–575

1. By **mutual** consent, the **musician** and his wife decided to move out of the **neighborhood** because the **moist** climate was lowering their **morale.**

2. Although the body of the **monarch** may **molder** beneath his **monument,** the **narrative** of his observations of the **nebula** will always be remembered by the **multitude.**

3. How the **monkeys** had escaped from the **municipal museum** would always remain a **mystery** to the **motorcycle** officers assigned to catch them.

4. **Moreover,** his **motive** in wishing to make us **nervous** by talking about a mysterious **monster** was not clear.

5. **Nevertheless,** the moral of the story is that **moisture** in tobacco will no more reduce **nicotine** than **mustard** will cure **nausea.**

576–600

1. **Numerous** members of the **organization** came to the **palace** for the **occurrence,** but **pandemonium** broke loose when the king failed to appear.

2. He had **originally** made the **observation** that to **ordain** a minister in an **opera** house was **outrageous,** and most people agreed.

3. **Obedient** though the **orphan** was, he had to offer **opposition** against the effort to **oppress** him for every minor **offense.**

4. It was a **novelty** for us to **observe** how the **oyster** would **occasionally nourish** itself.

5. To **operate** that **orchard** of **ours** allowed time for only an **occasional** trip to buy some clothing or an **ornament** for the house.

Advanced List Continued

551–575	576–600
moist	nourish
moisture	novelty
molder	numerous
monarch	obedient
monkeys	observation
monster	observe
monument	occasional
morale	occasionally
moreover	occurrence
motive	offense
motorcycle	opera
multitude	operate
municipal	opposition
museum	oppress
musician	orchard
mustard	ordain
mutual	organization
mystery	originally
narrative	ornament
nausea	orphan
nebula	ours
neighborhood	outrageous
nervous	oyster
nevertheless	palace
nicotine	pandemonium

Diagnostic Sentences

601–625

1. **Papa** was **partial** to **peanut** butter in his **pastry,** but in neither of the **pantries** could we find any.
2. People lining the **pavement** could **perceive** the look of the true **patriot** on the faces of the **parachute** troops who were passing in **parade.**
3. Every **paragraph** of the speech he delivered with such **passion** before **parliament** seemed like a **pearl** of wisdom dropped from **paradise.**
4. A good **percentage** of the horses stood **parallel** to one another in the **peaceful pasture,** looking as if they had been retired on **pension.**
5. His **patience** was rewarded when the **patent** office approved his **pattern** for a **penicillin** extractor and returned it by **parcel post.**

626–650

1. The great **persistence** a **pigeon** shows when it travels miles from its **perch** and returns is no **phenomenon** because I have **personally** seen it done.
2. No **phrase** in the **petition** demanded **perfection,** but it sought to **persuade** the governor to grant **permission** for action to be taken.
3. As he leaned against a **perpendicular pillar** near the **piazza** and breathed the **perfume** of the flowers, a pistol shot **pierced** the air.
4. Before the **picnicking** began, we thought we would **perish** from **perspiration,** but some **pineapple** juice followed by sandwiches and a **pickle** salad soon revived us.
5. Because his religious **philosophy** was not **permissible** at home, the **pilgrim** became a **pioneer** in search of **perpetual** freedom.

Advanced List Continued

601–625	626–650
pantries	perch
papa	perfection
parachute	perfume
parade	perish
paradise	permissible
paragraph	permission
parallel	perpendicular
parcel post	perpetual
parliament	persistence
partial	personally
passion	perspiration
pastry	persuade
pasture	petition
patent	phenomenon
patience	philosophy
patriot	phrase
pattern	piazza
pavement	pickle
peaceful	picnicking
peanut	pierced
pearl	pigeon
penicillin	pilgrim
pension	pillar
perceive	pineapple
percentage	pioneer

Diagnostic Sentences

651–675

1. One **premise** of modern **poetry** is that such common things as **potatoes** or **poultry** can become proper subjects for a **poem**.
2. **Preach** all he might about the value to **posterity** of the **preamble** to the Constitution, the **politician** still offered no **policy** to combat **pornography**.
3. She was **practically** mad about the **precious pottery** of the ancient **potentate** and showed her **preference** by outbidding everybody.
4. A **plunge** from the **platform** was no answer to her **poverty**, even though she had lost every **possession** to a convicted **polygamist**.
5. One should not **precede** the other, but public education and practical measures will prevent the **possibility** of a **pneumonia plague**.

676–700

1. Because I'm no **prophet**, I shall not **presume** to **prophesy** what **progress** you will make, but what I **prescribe** should help.
2. **Prominent** people considered it a **privilege** to lend their **presence** to the **procession** in honor of the **princess**.
3. **Probably** the old **principle** will be applied, and no one will **preside** over a **primary** election who has not had **previous** training.
4. The **proprietor**, a **prey** to wild schemes before, said there was no **prospect** he would accept this **proposition** without study and **preparation**.
5. Not to **prolong** his talk, the **principal** concluded with the **prophecy** that a large **proportion** of the graduates would **proceed** to college and do well.

Advanced List Continued

651–675	676–700
plague	preparation
platform	prescribe
plunge	presence
pneumonia	preside
poem	presume
poetry	previous
policy	prey
politician	primary
polygamist	princess
pornography	principal
possession	principle
possibility	privilege
posterity	probably
potatoes	proceed
potentate	procession
pottery	progress
poultry	prolong
poverty	prominent
practically	prophecy
preach	prophesy
preamble	prophet
precede	proportion
precious	proposition
preference	proprietor
premise	prospect

Diagnostic Sentences

701–725

1. There is no **question** that the **publication** will **qualify** for a higher rating when it makes **provision** to answer the charge of **racism.**
2. Every **reasonable** plan had been tried, and now only **Providence** would bring **prosperity readily** to the **realm.**
3. It was no **puzzle** why the people in the upper **province** did not protest over the **quarantine** because they had to **realize** that a possible epidemic was a **reality.**
4. **Psychology** tells us that **punishment** will not **quench** a strong spirit, but will merely **provoke** it to **pursue** its course all the harder. ·
5. The prosperous farmer enjoyed a high **protein** diet, but it was not a huge steak but a **rainbow** in the sky that could **quicken** his **pulse** with the sheer **rapture** of delight.

726–750

1. In his **replies,** the **representative** said he **regretted** that to **relieve** the situation there would have to be a **referendum** on changing the shape to a **rectangle.**
2. As no **remittance** of a **receipt** was made in my **remembrance,** we'll have to **relegate** the **remainder** of the balance to the accounts **receivable.**
3. To **recede** before public opinion meant to reject his ideals, and no man of **renown** could **renounce** his beliefs nor take **refuge** in fear.
4. If you reflect on what **remedy** will give you **release,** you will find that **religious** faith may **reconcile** you to your troubles.
5. Let us **rejoice** in the **reign** of this **remarkable** king who allows no **repetition** of the evils we had to **reckon** with before.

Advanced List Continued

701–725	726–750
prosperity	recede
protein	receipt
Providence	receivable
province	reckon
provision	reconcile
provoke	rectangle
psychology	referendum
publication	refuge
pulse	regretted
punishment	reign
pursue	rejoice
puzzle	release
qualify	relegate
quarantine	relieve
quench	religious
question	remainder
quicken	remarkable
racism	remedy
rainbow	remembrance
rapture	remittance
readily	renounce
reality	renown
realize	repetition
realm	replies
reasonable	representative

Diagnostic Sentences

751–775

1. To **rescue** Cárver was quite a **responsibility** because Gorman, **revolver** in hand, stood on a **ridge** and could easily **riddle** anyone who came near.
2. **Respective** doctors had told His **Reverence** that the pain seemed to **resemble rheumatism,** but he thought the idea **ridiculous.**
3. His **reputation** forced him to **resign** rather than **reverse** himself and **retreat** from a position he considered beyond **reproach.**
4. Because the decision of the **revenue** agent to tax your **reserve** fund is not **reversible,** thoughts of **revenge** will not **resolve** your difficulty.
5. Pancho **reveled** in the **restless** spirit of **resistance** that no one could **restrain** from becoming **revolutionary** in action.

776–800

1. We tried to be **sanitary,** but containers were **scarce** and we had to **rinse** out **salmon** or **sardine** cans and use them.
2. If the **rumor** that he had sold his **scheme** to the enemy were true, it would **ruin** the **scientist** and might cause a **riot.**
3. It must give that **rooster satisfaction** to keep his **schedule** because he will **rouse** us at dawn even on the Sabbath.
4. To call his **salve** a **sample** of the **sacred** ointment was bad enough, but to make it **salable** was **sacrilegious.**
5. On his **route** to the ranch, Chambers found a **savage** wild horse that took all his **science** to **saddle** in **satisfactory** fashion.

Advanced List Continued

751–775	776–800
reproach	rinse
reputation	riot
rescue	rooster
resemble	rouse
reserve	route
resign	ruin
resistance	rumor
resolve	Sabbath
respective	sacred
responsibility	sacrilegious
restless	saddle
restrain	salable
retreat	salmon
reveled	salve
revenge	sample
revenue	sanitary
reverence	sardine
reverse	satisfaction
reversible	satisfactory
revolutionary	savage
revolver	scarce
rheumatism	schedule
riddle	scheme
ridge	science
ridiculous	scientist

Diagnostic Sentences

801–825

1. A **sedative** and short rest on the **sofa** calmed the **seamstress** who had let out a **shriek** when the gas flame began **singeing** her hair.
2. Last **semester**, at the **settlement** house, a **socialist** delivered a **series** of talks, using a **simile** to describe how **sincerely** he felt.
3. With a **sigh**, Mr. Walton agreed with his friend, **Sergeant** Peters, that the painting **situated** in the social hall would have to be freshly **shellacked.**
4. The **shrewd** salesman was so **skillful** he could convince the most **sensible** that the **site** for their home was **similar** to the best.
5. All the **shepherd** did was **snatch** a pair of **shears** and cut the **slippery serpent** in two.

826–850

1. With a **solemn** nod, Mr. Ford revived Sally's **spirits** when he **specified** he would use enough **starch** to make her dresses **sparkle.**
2. We watched Mr. Gates **stalk** about the **stable** and **stare** at every corner because the **squirrel** was still **somewhere** around.
3. The **splendor** of a **spectacle** involving twenty **stately sopranos** singing together could **stagger** the imagination.
4. To **solve** the problem, he would tie every **solitary squash** to a **stake** and then **sprinkle** each with the insect powder.
5. Her **stationary** work and daily **solitude** made her study of the **sphere** to measure **spatial** relationships **somewhat** dull.

Advanced List Continued

801–825	826–850
seamstress	solemn
sedative	solitary
semester	solitude
sensible	solve
sergeant	somewhat
series	somewhere
serpent	sopranos
settlement	sparkle
shears	spatial
shellacked	specified
shepherd	spectacle
shrewd	sphere
shriek	spirits
sigh	splendor
similar	sprinkle
simile	squash
sincerely	squirrel
singeing	stable
site	stagger
situated	stake
skillful	stalk
slippery	starch
snatch	stare
socialist	stately
sofa	stationary

Diagnostic Sentences

851–875

1. Although **successful** in stealing **stationery** from the **studios**, he was too stupid to see he was **subtly** being allowed to develop a **superficial** sense of security.
2. The **substance** of the speech by the **superintendent** was that he would **strengthen** the strict application of the **statute** against wearing a **stethoscope** outdoors.
3. **Sulphur** fumes caused him to **stumble** on his way up the **steeple**, but his **stubborn** will was **sufficient** to keep him from falling.
4. Her sullen reaction to the **suggestion** by the **supervisor** to **stitch** the new pattern carefully was **suitable** reason for her dismissal.
5. As we made a **strategic** run through the **strait**, the crew had to **subdue** a **stowaway** who had tried to force the cook to **surrender** a jar of **strawberry** jam.

876–900

1. When **testimony** revealed that the **switchman** could not have been near the tavern, the **surrogate** showed some **sympathy** and resumed reading the will.
2. As if prompted by **telepathy,** we all proceeded to **surround** the **tannery** where the **teamster** worked and to hide in a **thicket** until the suspect came out.
3. **Symmetry** in design was no **temporary symbol** to the **textile** firms, but a permanent reminder that this would **sustain** their business.
4. To tease the **thirsty** boys, Sis poured some **syrup** into a glass and added milk, **thereby** making them mad with **temptation.**
5. When we **surveyed** the **temperature** on the **thermometer,** we realized that the use of **telemetry** to study the origin of a **tempest** in a **temperate** zone was a challenge to **terrestrial** observation.

Advanced List Continued

851–875	876–900
stationery	surrogate
statute	surround
steeple	surveyed
stethoscope	sustain
stitch	switchman
stowaway	symbol
strait	symmetry
strategic	sympathy
strawberry	syrup
strengthen	tannery
stubborn	teamster
studios	telemetry
stumble	telepathy
subdue	temperate
substance	temperature
subtly	tempest
successful	temporary
sufficient	temptation
suggestion	terrestrial
suitable	testimony
sulphur	textile
superficial	thereby
superintendent	thermometer
supervisor	thicket
surrender	thirsty

Diagnostic Sentences

901–925

1. In the **tragedy** of Caesar, we read how he returned in **triumph** and was **thrice** offered the **throne** by the Roman **throng.**
2. Whenever the **trumpet** announced a new **tributary** in the parade, it seemed to **torture** the **traitor** Cassius and make him **tremble** with rage.
3. Mr. Brice contracted **tonsillitis** trying to arrange **transportation** for every **trifle** contributed to swell the **treasury** of the **tuberculosis** fund.
4. We could **translate** the **twinkle** in the baron's eye as meaning he would forget the **tradition** of no **trespassing** on this lovely June **twilight.**
5. His **type** loved to **torment** others, and he would even **tread** on a **turtle** and **trample** it for the pleasure it gave him.

926–950

1. People would **vanish** into a secret **vault** under a **veil** of secrecy if they excited the **vengeance** of the old **tyrant.**
2. **Unfortunately,** in trying to keep the **ukulele underneath** the **umbrella,** Don dropped his **valise.**
3. **Ventilate** the room well because children **usually** regard the need to **vaccinate** them as **unnecessary tyranny** and are likely to faint.
4. His lack of **vanity** made him **uncertain** about how **usable** his **verse** would be, but it turned out to have **unexpected** merit.
5. When we did **venture** into the room, we found the **upholsterer,** almost **unconscious,** sitting **upright** on a pile of **velvet.**

Advanced List Continued

901–925	926–950
thrice	tyranny
throne	tyrant
throng	ukulele
tonsillitis	umbrella
torment	uncertain
torture	unconscious
tradition	underneath
tragedy	unexpected
traitor	unfortunately
trample	unnecessary
translate	upholsterer
transportation	upright
tread	usable
treasury	usually
tremble	vaccinate
trespassing	valise
tributary	vanish
trifle	vanity
triumph	vault
trumpet	veil
tuberculosis	velvet
turtle	vengeance
twilight	ventilate
twinkle	venture
type	verse

Diagnostic Sentences

951–975

1. Our study of the **videotape** showed that the **victorious warrior** used a trick **whereby** he was able to **whirl** the **villain** over his head and cast him down to defeat.
2. **Wherefore** such a **vulgar** display of **violence** arose over a slight **violation** of the order to "save a **watt**" was the ground **wherein** our complaint was lodged.
3. Far from the **wholesome** outer world, the **witch** retired into the **wilderness whither** she could **worship** her evil spirits.
4. **Whoever** sees **womenfolk** weave cloth in poor light should warn them of the weakness of **vision** that may result.
5. **Whew,** letting that part of the tube **wither** away is **voluntary** on your part, but I would **vulcanize** it with some **virgin** rubber.

976–990

1. Nothing could **wrinkle** the **worsted,** which was as soft as a spring **zephyr.**
2. So great was his **wrath** that the **wretched** boy would not **yield** though badly beaten.
3. A **wreath** was placed on the brow of the **yeoman** for his **zealous** performance of duty.
4. As a relief from his **zoological** studies, Terry took a cup of **yogurt** and stood near the **xylophone.**
5. If you believe in signs of the **zodiac,** those **zinnia** plants of **yours** will do well this year.

Advanced List Continued

951–975	976–990
victorious	worsted
videotape	wrath
villain	wreath
violation	wretched
violence	wrinkle
virgin	xylophone
vision	yeoman
voluntary	yield
vulcanize	yogurt
vulgar	yours
warrior	zealous
watt	zephyr
whereby	zinnia
wherefore	zodiac
wherein	zoological
whew	
whirl	
whither	
whoever	
wholesome	
wilderness	
witch	
wither	
womenfolk	
worship	

Sample Words*

from the
National Spelling Bee

Reprinted below are 480 words selected from the lists of over 3000 words found in "Words of the Champions," a practice booklet published by the National Spelling Bee.

FIRST ROUND

abbey	candied	famine
accomplice	canteen	filibuster
accumulate	category	flattery
acknowledge	celebrity	fossil
adhere	ceramics	furlough
affable	chop suey	
ambulatory		gallery
ammonia	denim	gladiator
artesian	desperate	groggy
attrition	destitute	gumption
austere	diagnosis	gutsy
	diaper	
beagle	dobbin	handicap
bonanza		hatchet
breadth	earring	hibiscus
brevity	edible	hitchhike
buckskin	extinct	homage

* Reprinted by permission of the National Spelling Bee, Scripps-Howard Newspapers.

illiterate
incriminate
injunction
innovate
issuance

jackknife
journey
justifiable

kangaroo
kernel
kindergarten

lectern
lesion

magnify
malice
mistletoe
multiplication

necessarily

nursery

ominous
onslaught
optimism

paraphrase
parity
permissive
personify
planetary
pontiff
pylon

quasi
quorum

relevant
riotous
rostrum

screech
secretive

segregate
semblance
squeamish
stampede

temporal
tentacle
terrain
testimony
thermal
triangular

ugliness
ultimate

vendetta
venerate

warrant
wastage
yawl
zenith

INTERMEDIATE WORDS

accrue
acerbity
acquittal
aggregate
alchemy
avalanche

bailiwick
barrio

bassoon
biennial
billiken

carcass
catamaran
cauliflower
charlatan
coalesce

condominium

dehydrate
dirigible
dischargeable
distillate
divestiture

elephantine

embryo
encompass
epochal
equilibrium
equipoise

fallible
feasible
fiendish
flourish

gaggle
glissade
gnome
guttural

haddock
hammock
harmonica
hoeing
hosanna

immature
indefensible
intermittent
interruption

jonquil
juggernaut

keenness
kinescope

lacrosse
laryngitis
limerick
livelihood

madonna
malapropism
mammary
martyrdom
mocha

necrology
neoclassicist
neurosis

oligarchy
omnipotence
ostensible

pancreas
persistent
petrochemical
pharaoh
prevaricator
psychological

quackery
quintuplet

raconteur
ramshackle
reciprocity
resistible

rheumatism
rhinoceros

sacrilege
schizoid
strategist
styptic
supersonic
sylph
symmetry

tabernacle
taciturn
thespian
transistor
trapezoid

unscrupulous
utterance

varicose
vengeance
veterinary

wheedle
windlass

yannigan
yoga

zircon
zouave

FINAL WORDS

aberration
abstemious
abysmal
acrimony
admonitory
allegretto
amanuensis
ambidextrous
anachronous
anaglyph
ancillary
antediluvian
apocalypse
apostrophe
apprehensible
arabesque
avaricious
avoirdupois

baccalaureate
bacchanalian
balbriggan
bamboozle
bathysmal
behemoth
blasphemy
bludgeon

cacophony
calamitous
calligrapher
camouflage
cannibalism

capillary
casuistry
catarrh
catechism
chandelier
chateaubriand
chauvinistic
chihuahua
chrysanthemum
cirrhosis
claustrophobia
cochineal
colloquialism
compatible
conglomerate
connoisseur
connubial
consummate
contretemps
coquettishly
corruptible
coterie

dactylic
daguerreotype
delicatessen
deluginous
demurrage
diaphanous
diaphragm
dichotomy
diphthong
dissonant

dithyramb
dossier
dysentery

ecclesiastical
effervesce
effluvium
eleemosynary
emollient
emphysema
encephalitis
ephemeral
equerry
erysipelas
espalier
eucalyptus
euphemism
eviscerate

farrago
flammable
flotsam
follicle
forfeiture
fricassee

geriatrics
guernsey
gyroscopic

haiku
harangue
hemophilia

hemorrhoid
hepatitis
horripilation
hyetology
hyperbole
hypochondriac

ichthyology
ignominy
impeccable
impecunious
imprimatur
inchoate
infinitesimal
insouciance
interregnum
irreconcilable
isosceles

jeremiad
jettisoned
jingoism

kaleidoscope
kamikaze
kleagle

lachrymose
lackadaisical
liquescent
logarithm

macrame
mademoiselle
maraschino
meerschaum
melancholia
metamorphosis

misogyny
mnemonic

nescience
nonagenarian
nouveau

obeisance
odoriferous
omniscience
opalescent
ophelimity
ophthalmic
oscillation

pachyderm
panegyric
panoplied
paradigms
paraphernalia
paroxysm
peccadillo
phalanx
photomontage
photosynthesis
phthalate
pirouette
plenipotentiary
poliomyelitis
prestidigitator
procrustean
proscenium
psilophyton
psoriasis
puissance
pusillanimous
pyrrhic

quadrennial
quintessence

ratiocination
recrudescence
rejuvenescence
renaissance
resuscitate
rhapsodical
rhododendron

saccharine
saprophagous
saurian
schizophrenia
semaphore
serendipity
soubrette
statuesque
stichometry
strychnine
stygian
surveillance
sycophant
syllepsis

testaceous
therapeutic
tintinnabulation
tonsillitis
trichinosis
turgescence

ubiquitous

valetudinarian

verdigris whimsicality xylophone
verisimilitude whippoorwill
vichyssoise whirligig zephyr
vignette zoological

WINNING WORDS

Here are thirty of the words on which national championships have been won or lost since the National Spelling Bee began:

abbacy	esquamulose	propylaeum
abrogate	eudaemonic	psychiatry
acquiesced	gladiolus	sacrilegious
afflatus	hydrophyte	sanitarium
asceticism	interning	semaphore
brethren	larghetto	sycophant
canonical	oligarchy	syllepsis
cinnabar	onerous	therapy
condominium	pronunciation	transept
croissant	propitiatory	uncinated

CAN YOU SPELL THESE?

The fate of fifty contestants in National Spelling Bee championship finals was determined by these fifty words:

aeriferous	cuisine	febrile
amaryllis	dilettante	flocculent
barycenter	distichous	fuliginous
beguine	edelweiss	geophagy
carioca	efflorescence	gneiss
cholesterol	elision	guyot
cincture	eschatology	homiletic
collodion	exacerbate	imitator

indissoluble	noblesse	scintillate
insouciant	ochlocracy	sericeous
jocose	orrery	stanchion
ligustrum	palilalia	syzygy
manumit	peripatetic	termagancy
medallion	peroration	vinegarroon
metonymy	potiche	weimaraner
minatory	quirt	xylophagous
nihilism	saponaceous	

THE LAST ROUNDUP

Here are one hundred of the most commonly misspelled words in the English language. If you score about 50 percent, you are in the average class; 60–70 percent, good; 70–85 percent, superior. Anyone who scores above 90 percent ranks in the top 1 percent of the population.

In each set below, only one of the words is spelled correctly. *Underline* the ones you think are right. Check your results with the answers that follow the list.

allotted–alloted	conquer–conquor
anoint–annoint	consistant–consistent
assinine–asinine	colossal–collosal
accomodate–accommodate	chagrined–chagrinned
accessible–accesible	changeable–changable
affidavit–affadavit	defanite–definite
all right–alright	desiccate–dessicate
apochryphal–apocryphal	desparate–desperate
arguement–argument	development–developement
ballistics–balistics	dilettante–dilletante
batallion–battalion	diphtheria–diptheria
benefited–benefitted	discernible–discernable
catagory–category	disheviled–disheveled
concensus–consensus	dissapate–dissipate
competent–competant	dissapoint–disappoint

disservice–diservice
dromedary–dromadery
drunkeness–drunkenness
ecstacy–ecstasy
embarrass–embarass
esophagous–esophagus
exhilarated–exilerated
exhorbitant–exorbitant
friccasee–fricassee
grievance–grievence
harass–harrass
hemorrage–hemorrhage
hygiene–hygene
hypocracy–hypocrisy
inadvertent–inadvertant
incalculable–incalcable
independent–independant
indispensible–indispensable
inflammation–inflamation
inimitable–inimatible
innoculate–inoculate
insistence–insistance
iridescent–iridecent
ireligious–irreligious
irresistible–iresistable
liquify–liquefy
lonliness–loneliness
macaber–macabre
mathematics–mathamatics
millionaire–millionnaire
missile–misile
misspelled–mispelled
naptha–naphtha
nickel–nickle
occassional–occasional
occurred–occured

parafernalia–paraphernalia
parallel–paralell
parrafin–paraffin
permissible–permissable
perseverence–perseverance
persistent–persistant
persue–pursue
predictable–predictible
proffesor–professor
propeller–propellar
protuberance–
   protruberance
questionnaire–questionaire
queue–quey
rarefy–rarify
recommend–reccommend
recconoiter–reconnoiter
rehearsal–rehersal
repitition–repetition
resistance–resistence
sacrilegious–sacriligious
seive–sieve
seige–siege
sieze–seize
separate–seperate
solitary–solitery
stratejacket–straitjacket
stupefy–stupify
supercede–supersede
supprise–surprise
surveillance–survalence
tenticles–tentacles
uncontrollable–
   uncontrolable
wierd–weird
zoology–zology

ANSWERS: allotted, anoint, asinine, accommodate, accessible, affidavit, all right, apocryphal, argument, ballistics, battalion, benefited, category, consensus, competent, conquer, consistent, colossal, chagrined, changeable, definite, desiccate, desperate, development, dilettante, diphtheria, discernible, disheveled, dissipate, disappoint, disservice, dromedary, drunkenness, ecstasy, embarrass, esophagus, exhilarated, exorbitant, fricassee, grievance, harass, hemorrhage, hygiene, hypocrisy, inadvertent, incalculable, independent, indispensable, inflammation, inimitable, inoculate, insistence, iridescent, irreligious, irresistible, liquefy, loneliness, macabre, mathematics, millionaire, missile, misspelled (*Did you see this in the opening paragraph?*), naphtha, nickel, occasional, occurred, paraphernalia, parallel, paraffin, permissible, perseverance, persistent, pursue, predictable, professor, propeller, protuberance, questionnaire, queue, rarefy, recommend, reconnoiter, rehearsal, repetition, resistance, sacrilegious, sieve, siege, seize, separate, solitary, straitjacket, stupefy, supersede, surprise, surveillance, tentacles, uncontrollable, weird, zoology.

Index

Instruction Guide for Teachers

Six Minutes a Day to Perfect Spelling combines the best of contemporary thinking in the field of spelling instruction with original suggestions and devices prepared by the author. Basically, the guiding pedagogic principle is the "test-study-test" approach, which is designed to diagnose the errors, adopt remedial measures, and examine the results of the learning process.

The book concentrates its attention largely on how the poor speller can most effectively overcome his difficulties by a method of study which makes words "part of him." There is, too, an abundance of diagnostic and testing material, both in the sentences found in the Appendix and the paragraphs used as chapter summaries.

Since the word lists have been graded, the use of the book is not restricted to any one school level. The "Basic Word List" contains samples that are suitable for elementary and junior high school students, the "Average List" for junior and senior high school classes, and the "Advanced List" for as high as the university level, where the author used it extensively with adult groups. The words were collated from existing scientific studies, state syllabi, school texts, and college surveys.

Every teacher of spelling undoubtedly has pet devices which have proved useful in the past, and we do not presume that the suggestions that follow are the definitive answers to the very real problem our youngsters face as they try to master our rather inconsistent language. However, the proposed methods of using the material have been carefully checked in classroom situations, and should serve certainly as *additional* means of realizing our common objective.

Listed here are ideas that can be used with the book:

✓Almost all authorities agree that it is undesirable to spend full periods on spelling. Rather it should be taught functionally, as the need arises with the individual student, or in short, frequently-spaced lessons. Both the "Daily Plan" and "Long Range Plan" should fit into this system very well. The teacher can utilize the suggested notebook arrangement and word-accumulation plan on a class as well as individual basis.

✓Possibly the chart found in the "Thirty-Day Trial" can become a permanent outline on a side blackboard, and be used for daily entry of particular problem words. The youngsters can devote three minutes in the morning, during the home room period, to their first atack on the word; can be encouraged to spend a second few minutes with the SEE-THINK-FEEL system during their study periods; and be assigned further to complete their third study of the word at home. Some students, preferably the better ones who do not need extensive drill, can be asked to volunteer to compose practice sentences and paragraphs containing the words listed in the daily chart described above. This approach offers motivation at all levels, and provides the teacher readily with testing material prepared by the students themselves.

✓As additional extra-credit work, students (in this case preferably the weaker ones) can be asked to bring in colored charts showing problem words presented as suggested in the chapter on "See the Word."

✔Occasionally, a few minutes can be spent asking the class to come up with a good "bond" for a word (See "Think the Word"). Some recognition may be given the ones who supply the best association patterns.

✔The better students may be assigned the task of helping others, especially in the reading of test paragraphs, the guiding of "Tracing" drills (See "Feel the Word"), and the marking of results.

✔The "spellagrams" can be fun for the youngsters, and it is suggested that the team games mentioned in the chapter on spelling games become regular parts of classroom routine. A league within a class may even be formed, daily contests held, and league standings posted prominently where the day-to-day won and lost records can be followed with interest by the contestants.

✔The chapter on word histories can be the springboard for adventures in words. Pupils who prepare little etymological stories can combine with others who have talent in art work. Some highly striking illustrations can be prepared. For example, one person may, let us say, draw a picture of Tantalus surrounded by water and overhanging branches of fruit, another prepare the story behind the name, and a third do the lettering of a typical derived word (*tantalize*), thus explaining why the problem A after the second T exists.

✔With the present interest in audio-visual aids, some thought can be given to the preparation of slides for projection. These can be used with the "See the Word" technique. Recordings, as indicated by Spellick #2, can be made of sample sentences and paragraphs. This can become a joint undertaking of the English and Speech departments. The resultant novelty and uniformity of presentation of test material to the classes will create added interest, besides relieving the teacher of the burden of dictation.

✔An interesting schoolwide project can be tried. The English Department can determine what ten words are most troublesome within each grade. A poster contest can then be initiated providing for entries within the grades, followed by competition among them all. Prizes can be awarded to grade winners as well as to the top three in the school. Many of the posters can be attached in rotating order to the bulletin boards in the classrooms, and the grand prize winners' entries can be hung in the school lobby or corridors. A mass program of this kind might well motivate better spelling among students of the entire school.

✔The industrial arts or shop departments may be willing to integrate their work with the English Department by permitting poor spellers to construct various "spellicks" as part of their required work for the term. These students can receive a mark from the shop teacher for the quality of their construction, and be further rewarded by the English teacher for making the effort to improve their spelling.

Insofar as the use of the book as a unit is concerned, the author wishes to recommend a procedure which, so far as he knows, is not in use in any of the schools. Teachers know, of course, that for some years considerable attention has been paid to remedial reading. Admittedly the problem in this area is extensive and demands concerted effort on the part of the educators. It is the opinion of the author, however, that there is an equally large number of students who need help in spelling. Schools might well consider the advisability of setting up *remedial spelling classes* in the same manner as reading groups are formed. A full term devoted to the practices outlined in *Six Minutes a Day to Perfect Spelling* should be rewarding for those who may otherwise pass on to adulthood with poor spelling plaguing their writing efforts.

In classes where poor spellers are in the minority, students may be advised to get the book and work with the more expert writers. A daily review of one word can be worked into the schedule. The pupil "teacher" can dictate a trial sentence while the attendance is being taken, in this way testing the results of the poor speller's study the previous day.